Modernism and ...

C000125540

Series Editor: Roger Griffin, Profess
University, UK

The series *Modernism and*... invites expe[...]g [...], [...], [...]
tific and political phenomena to explore the relationship between a particular topic in
modern history and 'modernism'. Apart from their intrinsic value as short but ground-
breaking specialist monographs, the books aim through their cumulative impact to
expand the application of this highly contested term beyond its conventional remit of
art and aesthetics. Our definition of modernism embraces the vast profusion of creative acts, reforming initiatives and utopian projects that, since the late nineteenth
century, have sought either to articulate, and so symbolically transcend, the spiritual malaise or decadence of modernity, or to find a radical solution to it through a
movement of spiritual, social and political – even racial – regeneration and renewal.
The ultimate aim is to foster a spirit of transdisciplinary collaboration in shifting the
structural forces that define modern history beyond their conventional conceptual
frameworks.

Titles include:

Roy Starrs
MODERNISM AND JAPANESE CULTURE

Marius Turda
MODERNISM AND EUGENICS

Shane Weller
MODERNISM AND NIHILISM

Ben Hutchinson
MODERNISM AND STYLE

Anna Katharina Schaffner
MODERNISM AND PERVERSION

Thomas Linehan
MODERNISM AND BRITISH SOCIALISM

David Ohana
MODERNISM AND ZIONISM

Richard Shorten
MODERNISM AND TOTALITARIANISM
Rethinking the Intellectual Sources of Nazism and Stalinism, 1945
to the Present

Agnes Horvath
MODERNISM AND CHARISMA

Erik Tonning
MODERNISM AND CHRISTIANITY

Forthcoming titles:

Maria Bucur
MODERNISM AND GENDER

Frances Connelly
MODERNISM AND THE GROTESQUE

Elizabeth Darling
MODERNISM AND DOMESTICITY

Matthew Feldman
MODERNISM AND PROPAGANDA

Alex Goody
MODERNISM AND FEMINISM

Carmen Kuhling
MODERNISM AND NEW RELIGIONS

Patricia Leighten
MODERNISM AND ANARCHISM

Paul March-Russell
MODERNISM AND SCIENCE FICTION

Ariane Mildenberg
MODERNISM AND THE EPIPHANY

Mihai Spariosu
MODERNISM, EXILE AND UTOPIA

Also by Erik Tonning

SAMUEL BECKETT'S ABSTRACT DRAMA: Works for Stage and Screen 1962–1985

SIGHTINGS: Selected Literary Essays by Keith Brown (*editor*)

BROADCASTING IN THE MODERNIST ERA (*with Matthew Feldman and Henry Mead*)

Modernism and ...
Series Standing Order ISBN 978–0–230–20332–7 (Hardback)
978–0–230–20333–4 (Paperback)
(*outside North America only*)

You can receive future titles in this series as they are published by placing a standing order. Please contact your bookseller or, in case of difficulty, write to us at the address below with your name and address, the title of the series and the ISBN quoted above.

Customer Services Department, Macmillan Distribution Ltd, Houndmills, Basingstoke, Hampshire RG21 6XS, England

MODERNISM AND CHRISTIANITY

Erik Tonning

Department of Foreign Languages, University of Bergen, Norway

For Matthew,

On the day of your
baptism; for my dear
brother in Christ, my
dearest colleague, my
friend. God bless
you, and thanks for
your rich contributions
to this small book.

Erik
York, 8 June 2014

palgrave
macmillan

First published 2014 by
PALGRAVE MACMILLAN

Palgrave Macmillan in the UK is an imprint of Macmillan Publishers Limited,
registered in England, company number 785998, of Houndmills, Basingstoke,
Hampshire RG21 6XS.

Palgrave Macmillan in the US is a division of St Martin's Press LLC,
175 Fifth Avenue, New York, NY 10010.

Palgrave Macmillan is the global academic imprint of the above companies
and has companies and representatives throughout the world.

Palgrave® and Macmillan® are registered trademarks in the United States,
the United Kingdom, Europe and other countries.

ISBN 978–0–230–24176–3 hardback
ISBN 978–0–230–24177–0 paperback

This book is printed on paper suitable for recycling and made from fully
managed and sustained forest sources. Logging, pulping and manufacturing
processes are expected to conform to the environmental regulations of the
country of origin.

A catalogue record for this book is available from the British Library.

A catalog record for this book is available from the Library of Congress.

For Tobias and Nathaniel

CONTENTS

Conclusion:
Modernism and Christianity as a Field of Study   124

SERIES EDITOR'S PREFACE

As the title 'Modernism and . . .' implies, this series has been conceived in an open-ended, closure-defying spirit, more akin to the soul of jazz than to the rigor of a classical score. Each volume provides an experimental space allowing both seasoned professionals and aspiring academics to investigate familiar areas of modern social, scientific or political history from the defamiliarizing vantage point afforded by a term not routinely associated with it: 'modernism'. Yet this is no contrived make-over of a clichéd concept for the purposes of scholastic bravado. Nor is it a gratuitous theoretical exercise in expanding the remit of an 'ism' already notorious for its polyvalence – not to say its sheer nebulousness – in a transgressional fling of postmodern *jouissance*.

Instead this series is based on the *empirically* oriented hope that a deliberate enlargement of the semantic field of 'modernism' to embrace a whole range of phenomena apparently unrelated to the radical innovation in the arts it normally connotes will do more than contribute to scholarly understanding of those topics. Cumulatively the volumes that appear are meant to provide momentum to a perceptible paradigm shift slowly becoming evident in the way modern history is approached. It is one which, while indebted to 'the cultural turn', is if anything 'post-post-modern', for it attempts to use transdisciplinary perspectives and the conscious clustering of concepts often viewed as unconnected – or even antagonistic to each other – to consolidate and deepen the reality principle on which historiography is based, not flee it, to move closer to the experience of history of its actors, not away from it. Only those with a stunted, myopic (and actually *unhistorical*) view of what constitutes historical 'fact' and 'causation' will be predisposed to dismiss the 'Modernism and . . .' project as mere 'culturalism', a term which due to unexamined prejudices and sometimes sheer ignorance has, particularly in the vocabulary of more than one eminent 'archival' historian, acquired a reductionist, pejorative meaning.

'Modernism' is a familiar term in debates between the 'conservative' and 'progressive' wings of various Christian denominations on such issues as homosexuality, contraception, ecumenicalism and the ordination of women. However, the subject of *Modernism and Christianity* is different, namely how the radical experimentation with new aesthetics and visions of a different type of social ethos associated with modernism in the early twentieth century were reflected in Christianity and how Christianity came to play an active role in some of those experiments. As such, even some open-minded readers may find the title of this book disconcerting. Like all the volumes in the series, it may seem to conjoin two phenomena that do not 'belong', in this case a secular cultural category with a religious belief system. However, any 'shock of the new' induced by the widened usage of modernism to embrace non-aesthetic phenomena that makes this juxtaposition possible should be mitigated by realizing that in fact it is neither new nor shocking. The conceptual ground for a work such as *Modernism and Christianity* has been prepared for by such seminal texts as Marshall Berman's *All That Is Solid Melts into Thin Air: The Experience of Modernity* (1982), Modris Eksteins's *Rites of Spring* (1989), Peter Osborne's *The Politics of Time: Modernity and the Avant-garde* (1995), Emilio Gentile's *The Struggle for Modernity* (2003) and Mark Antliff's *Avant-Garde Fascism: The Mobilization of Myth, Art and Culture in France, 1909–1939* (2007). In each case modernism is revealed as the long-lost sibling (twin or maybe even father) of historical phenomena from the social and political sphere rarely mentioned in the same breath.

Yet the real pioneers of such a 'maximalist' interpretation of modernism were none other than some of the major aesthetic modernists themselves. For them the art and thought that subsequently earned them this title was a creative force – passion even – of revelatory power which, in a crisis-ridden West where *anomie* was reaching pandemic proportions, was capable of regenerating not just 'cultural production', but 'socio-political production', and for some even society *tout court*. Figures such as Friedrich Nietzsche, Richard Wagner, Wassily Kandinsky, Walter Gropius, Pablo Picasso and Virginia Woolf never accepted that the art and thought of 'high culture' were to be treated as self-contained spheres of activity peripheral to – and cut off from – the main streams of contemporary social and political events. Instead they assumed them to be laboratories of visionary thought vital to the spiritual salvation of a world being systematically drained of higher meaning and ultimate purpose by the dominant, 'nomocidal' forces of modernity. If we accept Max Weber's thesis of the gradual *Entzauberung*, or 'disenchantment', of the world through rationalism, such creative individuals can be seen as setting themselves the task – each in his or her own idiosyncratic way – of *re-enchanting* and re-sacralizing the world. Such modernists consciously sought to restore a sense of higher purpose, transcendence and *Zauber* (magic) to a spiritually starved modern humanity condemned by 'progress' to live in a permanent state of existential exile, of *liminoid transition*, now that the forces of the divine seemed to have withdrawn in what Martin Heidegger's muse, the poet Friedrich Hölderlin, called 'The Flight of the Gods'. If the hero of modern popular nationalism is the Unknown Warrior, perhaps the patron saint of modernism itself is *Deus Absconditus*.

Approached from this oblique angle modernism is thus a revolutionary force, but is so in a sense only distantly related to the one made familiar by standard accounts of the (political or social) revolutions on which modern historians cut their teeth. It is a 'hidden' revolution of the sort referred to by the 'arch-'aesthetic modernist Vincent Van Gogh musing to his brother Theo in his letter of 24 September 1888 about the sorry plight of the world. In one passage he waxes ecstatic about the impression made on him, by the work of another spiritual seeker disturbed by the impact of 'modern progress', Leo Tolstoy:

> It seems that in the book, *My Religion*, Tolstoy implies that whatever happens in a violent revolution, there will also be an inner and hidden revolution in the people, out of which a new religion will be born, or rather, something completely new which will be nameless, but which will have the same effect of consoling, of making life possible, as the Christian religion used to.
>
> The book must be a very interesting one, it seems to me. In the end, we shall have had enough of cynicism, scepticism and humbug, and will want to live – more musically. How will this come about, and what will we discover? It would be nice to be able to prophesy, but it is even better to be forewarned, instead of seeing absolutely nothing in the future other than the disasters that are bound to strike the modern world and civilization like so many thunderbolts, through revolution, or war, or the bankruptcy of worm-eaten states.
>
> (Van Gogh 2003: 409)

In the series 'Modernism and . . .' the key term has been experimentally expanded and 'heuristically modified' to embrace any movement for change which set out to give a name and a public identity to the 'nameless' and 'hidden' revolutionary principle that Van Gogh saw as necessary to counteract the rise of nihilism. He was attracted to Tolstoy's vision because it seemed to offer a remedy to the impotence of Christianity and the insidious spread of a literally soul-destroying cynicism, which if unchecked would ultimately lead to the collapse of civilization. Modernism thus applies in this series to all concerted attempts in any sphere of activity to enable life to be lived more 'musically', to resurrect the sense of transcendent communal and individual purpose being palpably eroded by the chaotic unfolding of events in the modern world even if the end result would be 'just' to make society physically and mentally healthy.

What would have probably appalled Van Gogh is that some visionaries no less concerned than him by the growing crisis of the West sought a manna of spiritual nourishment emanating not from heaven, nor even from an earthly beauty still retaining an aura of celestial otherworldliness, but from strictly secular visions of an alternative modernity so radical in its conception that attempts to enact them inevitably led to disasters of their own following the law of unintended consequences. Such solutions were to be realized not by a withdrawal from history into the realm of art (the sphere of 'epiphanic' modernism), but by applying a utopian artistic, mythopoeic, religious or technocratic consciousness to the task of harnessing the dynamic forces of modernity itself in such spheres as politics, nationalism, the natural sciences and social engineering in order to establish a new order and a 'new man'. It is initiatives conceived in this 'programmatic' mode of modernism that the series sets out to explore. Its results are intended to benefit not just a small coterie of like-minded academics, but mainstream teaching and research in modern history, thereby becoming part of the 'common sense' of the discipline even of self-proclaimed 'empiricists'.

Some of the deep-seated psychological, cultural and 'anthropological' mechanisms underlying the future-oriented revolts against modernity here termed 'modernism' are explored at length in my *Modernism and Fascism: The Sense of a Beginning under Mussolini and Hitler* (2007). The premise of this book could be taken to be Phillip Johnson's assertion that 'Modernism is typically defined as the condition that begins when people realize God is truly dead, and we are therefore on our own' (Johnson 2013). It presents the well-springs of modernism in the primordial human need for a new metaphysical centre in a radically decentred reality, for a new source of transcendental meaning in a godless universe, in the impulse to erect a 'sacred canopy' of culture which not only aesthetically veils the infinity of time and space surrounding human existence to make existence feasible, but provides a totalizing worldview within which to locate individual life narratives, thus imparting it with the illusion of cosmic significance. By eroding or destroying that canopy, modernity creates a protracted spiritual crisis which provokes the proliferation of countervailing impulses to restore a 'higher meaning' to historical time, impulses that are collectively termed by the book (ideally and typically) as 'modernism'.

Johnson's statement seems to make a perceptive point by associating modernism not just with art, but with a general 'human condition' consequent on what Nietzsche, the first great modernist philosopher, called 'the Death of God'. Yet in the context of this series his statement requires significant qualification. Modernism is *not* a general historical condition (any more than 'post-modernism' is), but a generalized revolt against even the *intuition* made possible by a secularizing modernization that we are spiritual orphans in a godless and ultimately meaningless universe. Its hallmark is the bid to find a new home, a new community, and a new source of transcendence.

Nor is modernism itself necessarily secular. On the contrary, both the wave of occultism, theosophy and the Catholic revival of the 1890s and the emergence of radicalized, Manichaean forms of Christianity, Hinduism, Islam and even Buddhism in the 1990s demonstrate that modernist impulses need not take the form of secular utopianism, but may readily assume religious (some would say 'post-secular') forms. In any case, within the cultural force-field of modernism even the most secular entities are sacralized to acquire an aura of numinous significance. Ironically, Johnson himself offers a fascinating case study in this fundamental aspect of the modernist rebellion against the empty skies of a disenchanted, anomic world. A retired Berkeley law professor, some of the books he published, such as *The Wedge of Truth*, made him one of the major protagonists of 'Intelligent Design', a Christian(ized) version of creationism that offers a prophylactic against the allegedly nihilistic implications of Darwinist science.

Naturally no attempt has been made to impose the 'reflexive metanarrative' developed in *Modernism and Fascism* on the various authors of this series. Each has been encouraged to tailor the term modernism to fit their own epistemological cloth, as long as they broadly agree in seeing it as the expression of a reaction against modernity not restricted to art and aesthetics, and driven by the aspiration to create a spiritually or physically 'healthier' modernity through a new cultural, political and ultimately biological order. Naturally, the blueprint for the ideal society varies significantly according to each diagnosis of what makes actually existing modernity untenable, 'decadent' or doomed to self-destruction.

The ultimate aim of the series is to help bring about a paradigm shift in the way 'modernism' is generally used, and hence stimulate fertile new areas of research and teaching with an approach which enables methodological empathy and causal analysis to be applied even to events and processes ignored by or resistant to the explanatory powers of conventional historiography. I am delighted that Erik Tonning has taken the opportunity to show that while a driving force behind modernism was a sense of a growing spiritual crisis epitomized in the waning of Christian belief, Christianity could still be looked to by some major creative figures of the age as a remedy for the cultural crisis. In fact, this book is part of a major project he is leading to establish the complex patterns of 'de-' and 're-Christianization' that characterize a period in which the death of God turns out to have been greatly exaggerated.

ROGER GRIFFIN
Oxford
August 2013

PREFACE AND ACKNOWLEDGEMENTS

The idea for this study was first sparked when reading Keith Brown's fascinating account of Virginia Woolf's detailed use of Celtic myth as an alternative religious framework to Christianity in *Mrs Dalloway*, in an essay I later came to edit for his fine collection, *Sightings* (2008). I was particularly struck by the verbal comments on Brown's framework of interpretation made by Woolf's friend and close associate at the time of writing, Dr George Rylands:

> it does fit so well with the way I remember we were all talking, about that time: you know – feeling about for a replacement for Christianity. I know it perhaps sounds a little strange now [i.e. 1983], but the way things were then you simply couldn't conceive a world without *any* religion in it; but after the [1914–18] war Christianity, at least our Victorian gentle-Jesus kind, simply seemed to have nothing to offer.
>
> (quoted in Brown 2008: 226)

To feel about for a *replacement* religion, against a very specific cultural and religious context, and to deploy a complex alternative myth as part of a shadow-boxing match with Christianity taking place more or less beneath the surface of a major Modernist novel – all this struck me as significant far beyond Woolf's own case. It may seem strange to think this way now, as Rylands had remarked, but should not the scholar attempt historically to recover a time when even a Bloomsbury agnostic 'simply couldn't conceive a world without *any* religion in it' in order to trace the influences and creative pressures at work in individual cases?

This occurred to me in 2005, when I was finishing my doctorate on Samuel Beckett and also preparing to apply for a Norwegian Research Council postdoctoral grant. The topic of that grant application became 'Samuel Beckett and Christianity', and a survey of my perspective there may be found in Chapter 4 of this book. I am grateful to the Norwegian Research Council, the University of Oslo and the Centre for Christianity and Culture at Regent's Park College, Oxford for funding and hosting that research. In 2010, I was invited to apply for a broader research grant via the Department of Foreign Languages at the University of Bergen. I wish to thank my colleagues at Bergen, and former Bergen Professor Charles Armstrong in particular, for this opportunity, and the generosity of the Bergen Research Foundation (and its patron Trond Mohn) for making possible my current project called *Modernism and Christianity: Literature, History, Archive* (http://modernismchristianity.org). On that project, my colleagues Dr Matthew Feldman and Dr David Addyman have been superlative research partners, and my PhD students Jamie Callison, Jonas Kurlberg and Andrea Rinaldi are all producing work that will help to develop the field of 'Modernism and Christianity studies'. Again, I am grateful to the Bergen Department for facilitating this research and for welcoming me as a colleague. I also wish thank Professor Roger Griffin for inviting me to contribute to this book series, and the Palgrave editorial staff for their patience and professionalism.

Needless to say, the debts I have incurred along the way are very many. The following list reflects my profound gratitude to these individuals for commentary on my work, vital information, professional encouragement, personal support or all four, though of course, all remaining errors and omissions are my own: Chris Ackerley, David Addyman, Charles Armstrong, Mark Atherton, John Bolin, Leiv-Egil Breivik, Keith Brown, Mary Bryden, Daniela Caselli, Kelsey Conroy, Matthew Feldman, Paul S. Fiddes, Stefan Fisher-Høyrem, Finn Fordham, Roger Griffin, Fredrik Grønningsæter, Jostein Gundersen, Charles Hampton, Anne Hestnes, Suzanne Hobson, Fr Dominic Jacob, Anna Johnson, Randi Koppen, Jonas Kurlberg, Gregory Maertz, Henry Mead, Marjorie Perloff, Rosemary Pountney, Andrea Rinaldi, Lynn Robson, Gita Pattanaik Rongevær, Stuart Sillars, Are Skei, Anders Kristian Strand, Julian Thompson, Anne-Sissel Vedvik Tonning, Egil Tonning, Bjørn Tysdahl, Shane Weller, Janet Wilson, Nicholas Wood, Arve-Kjell Uthaug, Alette Vedvik, the late Einar Vedvik, Erna Vedvik, Ana Williamson, Timothy Williamson, and Judith Wolfe.

I wish to thank the Estate of T. S. Eliot (represented by Faber and Faber, Ltd), the Trustees of the David Jones Estate and the Trustees of the Ezra Pound Literary Property Trust (represented by New Directions Publishing Corporation) for kind permissions to quote from unpublished manuscripts. I am also grateful to Edinburgh

University Press for allowing me to reprint my article 'Beckett, Modernism, and Christianity' (forthcoming 2013 in S. E. Gontarski, ed., *The Edinburgh Companion to Samuel Beckett and the Arts*) as part of Chapter 4 of this book.

This book is dedicated to my sons, Tobias Einar Frederik Tonning and Nathaniel Jeremiah Tonning, with all my love.

LIST OF ABBREVIATIONS

See bibliography for full details of the editions used.

ACP	W. H. Auden, *Collected Poems*
APr II	W. H. Auden, *Prose: Volume II: 1939–1948*
APr III	W. H. Auden, *Prose: Volume III: 1949–1955*
APr IV	W. H. Auden, *Prose: Volume IV: 1956–1962*
DJDG	David Jones, *The Dying Gaul*
DJEA	David Jones, *Epoch and Artist*
DJIP	David Jones, *In Parenthesis*
ElCPP	T. S. Eliot, *The Complete Poems and Plays*
ElSE	T. S. Eliot, *Selected Essays*
EPCan	Ezra Pound, *The Cantos of Ezra Pound*
EPGK	Ezra Pound, *Guide to Kulchur*
EPPer	Ezra Pound, *Poetry and Prose: Contributions to Periodicals*
EPSP	Ezra Pound, *Selected Prose 1909–1965*
JJD	James Joyce, *Dubliners*
JJPA	James Joyce, *A Portrait of the Artist as a Young Man*
JJSH	James Joyce, *Stephen Hero*
JJU	James Joyce, *Ulysses*
SBCD	Samuel Beckett, *Complete Dramatic Works*
SBCP	Samuel Beckett, *The Complete Short Prose. 1929–1989*
SBDi	Samuel Beckett, *Disjecta*
SBDr	Samuel Beckett, *Dream of Fair to Middling Women*
SBDN	Samuel Beckett, *'Dream' Notebook*
SBHI	Samuel Beckett, *How It Is*
SBL1	Samuel Beckett, *Letters, Volume 1*
SBL2	Samuel Beckett, *Letters, Volume 2*
SBM	Samuel Beckett, *Murphy*
SBPD	Samuel Beckett, *Proust and Three Dialogues*
SBPo	Samuel Beckett, *The Collected Poems*
SBT	Samuel Beckett, *Molloy. Malone Dies. The Unnamable* ('Trilogy')
SBW	Samuel Beckett, *Watt*

1

RETHINKING 'MODERNISM AND CHRISTIANITY'

This book is about the formative and continuing impact of Christianity upon the cultural movement known as Modernism. It defends the view that any theoretical, historical or critical discussion of Modernism that neglects or minimizes that impact is inevitably flawed. The whole field of Modernism studies should thus be rethought in accordance with the insight that the role of Christianity is intrinsic to any coherent account of Modernism.

The full extent of such a task is plainly beyond the scope of a short volume such as this, and indeed beyond the field of expertise of any individual scholar. A major purpose of this book therefore is to pave the way for future work, ideally across the range of academic disciplines through which Modernism in the arts, in culture and even in politics has been examined. The present chapter will develop a theoretical argument for the centrality of Christianity to Modernism; the following three chapters contain case studies of six Anglophone Modernist writers in historical context; and the book's conclusion develops some implications for further study in the field of 'Modernism and Christianity'.

The Modernist Crisis

Central to the conception of Modernism adopted in this book is the idea that by the late nineteenth century, large numbers of artists, thinkers, and cultural and political ideologues and activists had begun to experience the condition of Western modernity as a crisis: a seemingly unprecedented period of transition or epochal transformation pointing to an unknown, perhaps a revolutionized, future.[1] The response to that crisis generated a panoply of experimental forms in the arts, alongside radical experiments in thought, living and politics as well. A Modernist, on this reading, is thus both on some level a theorist or thinker of cultural crisis, as well as a practitioner of experimental responses to that perceived crisis. The fundamental reason why Christianity is intrinsic to any coherent account of Modernism is that the very idea of an epochal cultural transformation at this time would necessarily involve some confrontation with the still-dominant religion and cultural paradigm of the West. How was the Christian past to be assessed? Was it worth preserving, or should it be overcome once and for all? How to relate to Christianity's present influence, both socially and individually? And did it have a future?[2] Whatever the answer, these questions could not be overlooked by Modernists. The overall strategy of this study is therefore to insert these questions into various existing accounts of Modernism and across the detailed case studies offered here, eschewing premature definitions but hoping to grasp some legs of the proverbial elephant by way of testing, probing and comparison.

A constant interlocutor in this book will be Roger Griffin's synoptic study *Modernism and Fascism: The Sense of a Beginning under Mussolini and Hitler* (2007). At the heart of Griffin's theory is the idea that Modernism arises out of a revolt against a late nineteenth-century *modernity*, increasingly constructed by artists and intellectuals – and after the First World War by much of the broader public radicalized by unprecedented carnage in Europe – as *decadence*. Modernity is of course itself a contested concept, but Griffin offers a suggestive list of criteria, citing

> the spread of rationalism, liberalism, secularization, individualism, and capitalism, the cult of progress, expanding literacy rates and social mobility, urbanization and industrialization, the emergence of the urban middle (capitalist) and working (rural and proletarian) classes from a feudal structure of society, the growth of representative government and bureaucratization, revolutionary developments in communications and transport, geographical discoveries and imperial expansion, the advance of secular science and ever more powerful technology and technocracy.
>
> (Griffin 2007: 46)

There is, Griffin points out, considerable scholarly consensus on the subjectively disorienting, destabilizing result of this historical process (47).[3] Furthermore, several scholars of modernity have noted how heightened self-reflexivity concerning humans as 'historical agents living within a unique constellation of historical forces' (49) early led to a widespread sense of the future as 'no longer a neutral temporal space for what destiny or providence will bring, but a site for realizing transformative cultural, social or political projects through human agency' (50).[4] This fuelled the Enlightenment and its revolutions, while also underpinning the more general nineteenth-century ideology of Progress. However, at some point a counter-reaction begins:

> In the decades after the largely abortive 1848 revolutions, in marked contrast to the French Revolutionary period that had made them possible, the quintessentially modern experience of contemporary history as opening out into an as yet undefined future, as permanently pregnant with an 'epochal new beginning', began to run *against* the grain of actually existing modernity and the way post-Revolutionary society was visibly developing. In this profoundly *uncoordinated*, heterogeneous, polycentric countermovement the orthodoxy of political and technocratic progress came to be rejected as constituting in itself a superseded and moribund 'tradition' that urgently demanded to be transcended in order to find new sources of meaning, spirituality and communality. (52)

On one hand, then, according to Griffin, 'actually existing modernity' is increasingly construed as spiritually empty, threatened by nihilism and a subjective threat of dissolution and *anomie*;[5] whereas on the other hand, the impulse to *overcome* this decadence is itself infused with 'epochal' thinking, wherein the future is seen as mouldable, and ripe for regeneration through 'creative destruction' (54). As this last term indicates, Modernism is complexly 'Janus-headed', expressing 'both cultural pessimism and optimism, moods of despair and celebration' (55): thus we find an ongoing 'dialectics of chaos and (new) order, despair and hope, decadence and renewal' (54). This then is the 'sense of a beginning' – or *Aufbruch* – alluded to in Griffin's title. As Griffin notes, such a Modernist stress on transcendence, revitalization or redemptive regeneration has long been aligned with apocalyptic thought: where the collapse of the Old Order inaugurates the New (55).[6]

For Griffin, crucially, Modernism is not simply a movement within the arts: he distinguishes between 'programmatic' or political Modernism, which aims for a total renovation and reconstruction of whole societies to produce a regenerated New Man and a new overarching structure of meanings for such a society to live by; and 'epiphanic' Modernism, meaning radically experimental modes of artistic expression aiming to elicit (however momentarily) some form of intensified visionary experience, a glimpse of transcendence to set against a looming cultural breakdown and the threat of *anomie*. His definition of Modernism is geared towards the analysis of generic fascism[7] as a form of Modernism. The ideology of fascism for Griffin is driven by *palingenesis*: 'projects of national, social, racial or cultural cleansing or rebirth' that were to be 'engineered through the power of the modern state' (8), while using myths and public 'liturgies' to present a semi-religious vision of the purified national community.

This book will touch on fascism in Chapters 2 and 3, but for present purposes, Griffin's emphasis on Modernism as involving a pronounced religious impulse is of special concern. For Griffin, the Modernist crisis develops out of the erosion by the forces of Western modernity of a sheltering 'sacred canopy',[8] meaning any stable system of collective meanings providing cultural value and some form of mythical significance to both individual and societal life. In its search for 'new sources of meaning, spirituality and communality', Modernism on this reading seeks to fill a need for religious significance: a drive towards 'redemption' or 'transcendence' viewed as intrinsic to humanity. While this characterization of Modernism as, in part, an alternative religious formation is useful and suggestive, the historical impact of Christianity upon Modernism is correspondingly overlooked because Christianity here becomes largely an inert thing of the past, simply that which can no longer provide a 'sacred canopy'. But this obscures the continuing influence of Christianity as a cultural and political force throughout the Modernist period. Any effort to overcome Christianity, and to invent alternative forms of transcendence in the late nineteenth to early twentieth century West, would still be costly and challenging for the individuals and movements concerned. Thus, the 'sense of a beginning' described by Griffin necessarily involved as well some definite stance on the past, present and future of Christianity in Western culture. The very idea of epochal transformation, in fact, involves a specific imaginative construction of the Old Era in contradistinction from the New. A fundamental task for 'Modernism and Christianity' as a field of study, therefore, is to chart and document how this active, unavoidable, *formative* tension manifests itself from case to case. In order properly to register the sheer weight of contextual pressure from the various incarnations of Christianity upon individual Modernist movements, life-stories and *oeuvres*, it is imperative to ask for dense historical context, archival research and biographical and textual details. Carefully tracing individual patterns of resistance or appropriation brings out the way characteristic themes tend to shape themselves *around* that tension. With this information to hand, the wider task of comparison between the many modes of Modernist creative response to Christianity can begin.

Another important focus for the study of 'Modernism and Christianity' that Griffin's framework helps to illuminate is the distinct phenomenon of *Christian Modernisms*, often involving converts or returns to the faith. While Griffin keeps Christianity very much in the background of his argument and does not mention this group, his emphasis on the element of revolt against a 'decadent' modernity in need of spiritual 'revitalization' nonetheless offers a way to integrate the idea of 'Christian Modernism' into the field of Modernist studies. Very simply, for *this* group of Modernists, a revived Christianity was precisely the tonic needed to regenerate a spiritually empty modern civilization. Of course, other Modernists who happened to see Christianity as antithetical to the New Era as they understood it were bound to perceive this attitude as inherently retrogressive and incomprehensible, as in Virginia Woolf's well-known outburst after a meeting with the recently converted T. S. Eliot:

> I have had a most shameful and distressing interview with poor dear Tom Eliot, who may be called dead to us all from this day forward. He has become an Anglo-Catholic, believes in God and immortality, and goes to church. I was really shocked. A corpse would seem to me more credible than he is. I mean, there's something obscene in a living person sitting by the fire and believing in God.[9]

Equipped with Griffin's framework, the scholar of Modernism can see that revitalization and transcendence[10] is very much at stake for *both* Woolf and Eliot, despite their differing ideologies. In Chapter 3, we will see how Eliot's attraction to Christian dogma was a direct response to a sense of profound cultural crisis and existential *ennui*;

although he may have seemed corpse-like to Woolf, he too was seeking an access of New Life by using dogma to articulate the necessity for the intrusion of the otherness of God into history in order to save civilization.

In Woolf's virulent response, one important role of Christianity in the genesis of some articulations of Modernism is evident: that of Grand Enemy. This then is one important kind of formative tension, and we shall see in Chapter 2 how resistance against the 'anti-Modernist' campaign of the Catholic Church could unite a broad range of mutually contradictory cultural ideologies under the counter-sign of *pro*-Modernism. Of the two case studies in that chapter, David Jones best fits the idea of a 'Griffinite Christian Modernist' as outlined in the previous paragraph, concerned as he is with cultural decadence and regeneration. Yet in contrast, the case of James Joyce presents a further complex conceptual challenge here. From one angle, it is not unreasonable to call him a 'Catholic' Modernist, in the sense of someone who (unlike, say, Woolf) was indelibly influenced in his work and thought by his encounter with the Catholic Church. On the other hand, he 'left the Catholic Church, hating it most fervently',[11] and it became for him a symbol of all that was deathly, stifling and unregenerate, not least in Irish society. But unlike Jones, Joyce did *not* construe modernity itself as the source of decadence: on the contrary, for him the church was at the root of society's sickness, and it is, paradoxically, the modern 'vivisective'[12] spirit that becomes associated with New Life in opposing that institution. Accordingly, while the broad 'apocalyptic' crisis pattern of decadence–revitalization identified by Griffin is arguably still at work here, Joyce's case suggests that for some Modernists at least, the church and not modernity per se remained the principal adversary. Here, then, is another reason to insist that the role of Christianity is intrinsic to a coherent account of Modernism.

Modernism and Christianity: Some Formative Tensions

While the chapters to follow will explore the work of three 'Christian Modernists' (Jones, Eliot and W. H. Auden), the present discussion will try to articulate the notion of formative tensions between Modernism and Christianity in further detail. These do not necessarily involve aggressive confrontation, though that is often enough the case. This section thus identifies three broad ideological clusters that were clearly influential upon Modernism – vitalism, occultism and the theme of a 'second Renaissance' or modern rebirth of classical antiquity – where further study of the formative tensions with Christianity seems both fruitful and necessary.[13]

In the cultural movement of 'vitalism', which was extremely influential across Europe around the turn of the twentieth century, we find a distinctive articulation of the broader Modernist drive towards 'revitalization' examined above.[14] Eirik Vassenden's recent study of this area offers an incisive guide here. Vassenden defines vitalism as centred on the idea that 'all life stems from a special Life Force, a creative impulse that is not explicable in terms of mechanical laws'; it further involves a tendency to 'worship force and vitality [...] as manifested in and through nature', and to value 'the instincts, intuition and the irrational above rational thought and the social contract' (Vassenden 2012: 13).[15] Vitalism may make use of science in an attempt to prove or access the Life Force, or it may oppose scientific categories in order to grasp 'life' more authentically through intuition (14). Some vitalists displayed an aversion to modern civilization and technology, whereas others celebrated technology as a fresh expression of the Life Force. Politically, there were links to the extreme right, for instance via the nature mysticism of the German *Blut und Boden* movement that ultimately fed into National Socialism, yet one also finds strains of anti-establishment rhetoric, anti-bourgeois leftism, pacifism and even anarchism (14). Despite such variations, an important common feature is a fascination with all things forceful, rapturous and overwhelming (14), as well as with transformation, movement or dynamism (22). Another overall trend is a certain incipient antihumanism, in that *life itself* is given primacy over *human life*; that is, the drive towards ecstatic union with the Life Force or cosmos tends to diminish the importance of the individual (36–7).

The impact of vitalism on natural philosophy and science at this time, and upon biology in particular, is sometimes neglected by cultural historians of this period. Yet in fact, as Peter J. Bowler has shown, the actual reception of Darwin both by scientists as well as in the broader culture tended to sideline the principle of natural selection (see Bowler 1988, ch. 4, on 'the eclipse of Darwinism' (92) by 1900). Instead, the emphasis fell upon a more teleological 'evolutionism', emphasizing morphological similarities across species as expressions of the very mould of Life, alongside a drive towards more complex, 'higher' species as pointing to an entelechy beyond the random selection of strict Darwinism. As both Bowler and Vassenden acknowledge, a key figure here is the German Zoologist Ernst Haeckel, whose widely popular books and lectures emphasized the aesthetic beauty of the fundamental forms and proportions of life (pre-eminently in *Kunstformen der Natur* (1899–1904)). He thus promoted *monism* as a 'bond between religion and science' or 'unity between God and the world' (in *Die Welträthsel* (1895–99) and *Die Lebenswunder* (1904)), albeit at a molecular and cellular level (Vassenden 2012: 23; see also Bowler 1988: 77–90). An emblem of the 'replacement religion' character of much vitalist evolutionism is the crowning of Haeckel as 'anti-pope' at the 1904 'Freethinker's Convention' in Rome.[16]

Moving from science to the arts, Vassenden identifies such typical vitalist motifs as the sun (with human bodies in free, natural activity in the sunlight), the blood and sexual play and reproduction – all signifying human immersion in the natural cycle (Vassenden 2012: 28). These joyous notes are counterpointed by motifs of violence, fighting, war, natural disaster, fire or lightning. Such extremes display the overpowering force and creative destruction inherent in Life, while also potentially cleansing and purifying the human world of all that is rigid, stale and over-civilized (29). In this way, vitalism in art connects with the more specific interests in primitivism, myth and the unconscious so prevalent at this time.

The two most influential philosophers of vitalism are Friedrich Nietzsche and Henri Bergson, who of course on any reading are also pivotal figures in the development of Modernism.[17] The Life Force in *Thus Spake Zarathustra* (1885) is named the Will to Power, and the emphasis is on competition, hierarchy and command. Creation, action and will are opposed to science, reason and the stale traditions inherited from history. This fiercely apocalyptic and prophetic book famously recommends an ultimate overcoming of 'man' himself, who is but a temporary 'bridge' towards the future *Übermensch*. Nonetheless, this apocalyptic development does not finally instigate any new Kingdom, but is itself merely part of an unending cycle, the perpetual return of the same. As Vassenden points out, Bergson's emphasis, by sharp contrast, is on the mutual sympathy or understanding between all living things; he also draws much more on orthodox science, and was a respected figure of the academic establishment. Bergson's focus is on memory and the subjective experience of time: '*La durée* is the connection between that which has been and that which is, but it also connects that which is to that which *will be*. Time is creation – life – in this sense' (Vassenden 2012: 77). Bergson thus distinguishes his philosophy from a mechanistic Darwinism on the one hand, and what he calls 'finalism' – meaning the creation-derived teleology of Christianity – on the other.

This dual distinction is an effective guide for further study of the relationship between vitalism and Christianity. Christianity consistently remains one of the poles against which distinction must be made, or towards which an anxious line must be drawn. This is even more obvious with Nietzsche, the son of a pastor and originally destined for the church, whose every work fulminates against what he came to call the Christian 'slave-mentality' and *ressentiment*.[18] A fruitful starting point for such study might be to focus on the many texts and artworks across the vitalist field dealing directly with Christianity in order to catalogue the types of response at work. A striking example here is D. H. Lawrence's last book, *Apocalypse* (1931), a vitalist reading of the Book of Revelation.[19] Lawrence opens by professing his loathing of the version of the Bible, and Revelation in particular, inculcated in the nonconformist chapel of his childhood. It was not simply read, but 'expounded dogmatically, and always morally expounded' (Lawrence 1977: 4), while 'the interpretation was fixed, so that all interest was lost' (4). By contrast, he goes on, a book only 'lives' whilst 'unfathomed' (4), and Lawrence's fiercely oppositional reading of St John's Apocalypse to find traces of an underlying pagan cosmology is precisely intended to sensitize modern-day readers – sealed within the isolated ego – to the text's metaphorical richness and mythical depth, thus reinvigorating the 'eternal vital correspondence' (29) between humanity and cosmos. A passionate rereading of the Apocalypse could thus point moderns to a New Era, for by the

> very frenzy with which the Apocalypse destroys the sun and the stars [...] we can see how deeply the apocalyptists are yearning for the sun and the stars and the earth and the waters of the earth, for nobility and lordship and might, and scarlet and gold splendour, for passionate love, and a proper unison with men, apart from this sealing business. (125)

Lawrence identifies two clashing tendencies within the text: a primary strain of glorious pagan myth – supposedly from an older manuscript redacted by John and later Christian scribes – and a secondary drive towards *ressentiment*, which laid the basis for 'the

Christianity of self-glorification: the self-glorification of the humble' (11). Lawrence's book therefore encapsulates nearly every theme of this chapter thus far, yet there are also any number of case studies with which to compare his work, across the areas sketched out here under the heading of vitalism.

One of the most significant interventions into the study of Modernism and religion in the past few decades has been the recognition of the impact of occultism, issuing in such invaluable studies as Leon Surette's *The Birth of Modernism: Ezra Pound, T.S. Eliot, W.B. Yeats and the Occult* (1993) and Alex Owen's *The Place of Enchantment: British Occultism and the Culture of the Modern* (2004). A similar insight to that developed in the treatment of vitalism above might ground future work on Modernism, Christianity and the occult: namely that occultists needed actively to distinguish their syncretic religion from materialism and Darwinism on the one hand, and from Christianity on the other. Clearly, examples of 'occultist' Modernist writing and thought dealing directly with Christian scripture, dogma, imagery or symbols would be the most natural starting points in mapping this field. For instance, a comprehensive study of the Christ figure and Christian symbolism in relation to the occult in W. B. Yeats's work is lacking.[20] Again, however, the larger task is to compare individual case studies in order to chart the varieties of 'formative tension' at work. The 'esoteric Christianity' expounded by individuals like the English theosophist Annie Besant and the Austrian anthroposophist Rudolf Steiner is another area of obvious interest here.

Beyond these general points, Leon Surette's study expounds an approach that implicitly underwrites the approach to 'Modernism and Christianity' adopted in this book. This is the theme of occult 'secret histories', seeking to recover a lost or hidden esoteric tradition of supposedly ancient wisdom and spiritual power, suppressed by the mainstream culture of the West, but visible at the margins of texts and historical movements, especially in the work of a select elite of enlightened individuals who form 'a kind of apostolic succession' (Surette 1993: 51) through the ages. Christianity typically figures in such histories as influential oppressor and prime antagonist:

> Occultism's claim to belong to a tradition much older than Christianity cannot be taken seriously. It is, in fact, an attempt to *recover* older, pagan beliefs and practices from *within* Christianity. It is for this reason that occultists characteristically attribute the survival of their cult to secret,

underground societies and are typically hostile to the Christian church and often to Christian beliefs as well. Their understanding of historical process tends to derive from the paradigmatic case of an archaic wisdom or practice suppressed – and often oppressed – by authorities committed to a degenerative or corrupt version of the true, pure, archaic faith. (50)

At the same time, this historical orientation is not merely antiquarian but distinctively Modernist, for these occultists 'frequently assert that the fragments have now, finally, been sufficiently recovered for the ancient wisdom to be reconstituted, making them appear to be modern progressive thinkers. One touchstone that can help to identify the occultist is his tendency to speak of a cultural "rebirth", "return", or *risorgimento*' (50). Surette then advances a principle that guides the present study, even if he does not explicitly highlight the centrality of the role of Christianity to Modernism *tout court* that is argued here: 'The one universal feature of modernism was its epochal thinking. All "ideologies" or "philosophies" defined themselves as either the end or the beginning of an era' (71).

One complex case of the interaction of occultist epochal thinking with the re-imagination of Christian history and dogma (surveyed in Chapter 3 of this book) is that of Ezra Pound, who is also a major focus of Surette's wider research. While Pound's occultism started from the kind of anti-Christian 'secret histories' described by Surette, there is also a period of his career as a Fascist propagandist for Mussolini's Italy (explicitly from about 1936) where he adopted a more welcoming, appropriative approach to the Catholic Church, claiming that aspects of the secret tradition of the Eleusinian mysteries had survived within the Church, and that the real 'Old Testament' of Christianity was not actually the Hebrew scriptures (supposedly tainted by Jewish 'usury'), but rather pagan antiquity itself.

The latter 'insight' stems from Pound's reading of the obscure Polish classicist Thaddeus Zielinski, whose *La Sybille* (1924) he thought important enough to recommend for translation and republication to Noel Stock after the Second World War, while he was still languishing in St Elizabeths Hospital. This small curiosity further underscores that the promotion of a revival of classical learning and culture in the Modernist period was rarely a mere question of antiquarianism. Indeed, as Jeffrey Perl points out, the idea of modernity as such 'has, since the Renaissance, been intimately tied to the notion of a classical rebirth', evident in the very ancient/medieval/modern scheme itself

(Perl 1984: 20). Furthermore, for the likes of Jacob Burckhardt in his influential study of the Italian Renaissance (1860), notes Perl, 'the twentieth century was meant to be a renascence of the Renaissance', a rebirth that would complete the earlier, abortive one: 'The bourgeois progressivism and technological novelty-seeking of the Protestant era seem[ed] to have little in common with the aristocratic, Latin institutions that Italian humanists had expected to revive and purify' (23).

In Burckhardt's scheme, the two 'middle' epochs – the medieval and the modern – were both rejected in favour of the historical 'Renaissance', and the anticipated *coming* classical rebirth:

> The middle epoch is rejected because its thinkers refused to accept man as he is – they insisted on theorizing and idealizing humanity. In reaction, Burckhardt endorses the Homeric Greeks' strong personalities, their refusal to recoil from the gruesome, their lack of inhibitions and guilt feelings, their easygoing response to bodily needs or desires, and their innocence of dividing passions.
>
> (Perl 1984: 24)

Perl also stresses that Burckhardt was Nietzsche's older colleague at Basel, and in *The Birth of Tragedy from the Spirit of Music* (1872) the younger man would praise the ecstatic intensities and mythic profundity of ancient tragedy, with its ritual use of the chorus, music and sonorous poetry. These works enabled the ancients to confront pain, dissolution and chaos, and still to rejoice in the world as 'aesthetic phenomenon'. Nonetheless, as Perl notes, 'Nietzsche's passionate attachment to artificial, classical verse-tragedy is [...] no mere aesthetic preference, and his assault on naturalist prose-drama is simultaneously an attack on an entire culture' (Perl 1984: 119), namely the 'bourgeois ethic of modernity [which] assumes that life is to be made as easy and regular as possible, leading the collectivized man from a hygienic birth to an anesthetized death' (118). Nietzsche would later blame Christian *ressentiment* for the ascendancy of this ethic. Once again, the call is for a return, a modern *re*-birth of tragedy from the spirit of music, symbolized at this stage in Nietzsche's career by Richard Wagner's music – though Nietzsche would break with Wagner over *Parsifal* (1882), which stood in his view for regression to Christian-ascetic ideals rather than renewal. Perl's study shows how this whole ideology of return-as-rebirth, or *nostos*, 'imposes a psychological structure upon [...] the history of culture' (30): 'Ideologists of return share the assumption that man possesses a unified sensibility, and the historical divisions they posit tend to correspond with supposed dissociations or reassociations in the cultural psyche' (25).

While Perl, like Surette, does not develop his insight beyond the specific ideology he is considering, he is still quite clear that this creative A–B–A patterning of cultural history in terms of once and future 'rebirth' (and promised psychic reintegration) involves an inevitable confrontation with Christianity:

> The central question faced by the modernists was, historically speaking, What is the meaning of the middle period? or, put in its more usual form, What is Christianity? What purpose did it or does it serve, and has it a future? In the twentieth century, we are all post-Christians, even if some of us – Eliot, for example, are Christians as well. We no longer *assume* Christianity. In general, the modernists attempt to deconstruct Christianity and its cosmology at the same time that they attempt to construct a post-Christian cosmology based on pre-Christian ones. The modernists tend to share constellations of objections to Christianity: it is life-denying (it centers on crucifixion), its view of human nature is incorrect (it cleaves the soul from the appetites), it is dangerously *telos*-oriented. The modernists demand, by and large, the opposite of these principles as guides for living, and they pair their fledgling post-Christian cosmology with venerable pre-Christian ones.
>
> (Perl 1984: 12–13)

One might demur that these generalized types of 'objection' hardly exhaust the possible relations at stake, and there is indeed plenty of scope for further work in juxtaposing Christianity and the Modernist drive for a second classical renaissance more systematically. However, this third type of formative tension between Modernism and Christianity – in its focus on the ideologically charged nature of the whole idea of modernity, and in the stress on an ongoing clash of 'cosmologies' – crucially raises a broader question that must now be confronted. How does one describe the role of Christianity in the development of that very condition of late nineteenth-century modernity which precipitated the Modernist crisis?

The Theological Origins of Modernity?[21]

To focus this question, it is convenient to start by distinguishing the approach to religion in Modernism taken in this study from that of Pericles Lewis in his fine monograph *Religious Experience and the Modernist Novel* (2010):

> In the same generation, the agnostic or atheistic authors discussed here sought to make the structure of the novel more capable of describing transcendent experiences. For the modernists, transcendence generally meant experiences that originated in the ordinary world, not the supernatural, but that opened some sort of insight beyond the realm of the ordinary; for such experiences they often used religious language, such as the term 'epiphany'. Without submitting to the institutional religion of church or synagogue, the modernists found methods to describe through fiction what came to be known, after William James, as 'religious experience', the basic consciousness supposedly at the root of all religions but isolated from any institutionalization in a theology or a church.
>
> (Lewis 2010: 19–20)

The problem here is that in arguing for a sort of migration of 'religious experience' from a previous religious language (that of Christianity or Judaism) into the Modernist novel, Lewis willingly adopts the Jamesian concept of religious experience for the purposes of his own analysis.[22] Yet that seemingly neutral concept is itself a specific late nineteenth-century invention, *actively wrested by James from the background of a Christian theological matrix.*

It is instructive then to take a closer look at the Jamesian category of religious experience, that 'basic consciousness supposedly at the root of all religions', as Lewis puts it. In an indispensable article, Leigh Eric Schmidt ties this category directly to the nineteenth-century 'invention of mysticism as the fountainhead of all genuine spirituality' (Schmidt 2003: 281), a 'universal quintessence of religious experience' (276) common to both East and West. Schmidt traces the genealogy of the word 'mystical' in English: from its application to 'mystical theology' simply as a branch of Christian devotion emphasizing contemplation, or alternatively as denoting biblical exegesis in search of hidden spiritual meanings; via its use in the deistic and rationalist climate of the eighteenth century as a stick with which to beat 'enthusiasm' in religion; and on to the view enshrined in the 1797 *Encyclopædia Britannica* that the 'mystics', so far from tapping into any global quintessence, were marginal sectarians, such as the Quietists, the Quakers and the Methodists. This throws into relief the considerable creative effort needed to new-mint this term for modern uses: 'In Transcendentalist hands the term was clearly being dislodged from both its Catholic and its Enlightenment roots. It was neither an ancient form of Christian divinity nor part of a critique of enthusiasm and sectarianism; instead it was becoming loosely spiritual, intuitive, emancipatory, and universal' (286). James's *The Varieties of Religious Experience* (1902) is unmistakably rooted in just this New England Transcendentalism, which sought an 'intellectual shield against untrammelled naturalism' (287), while being deeply engaged in 'a particular set of cultural negotiations over the reality and unreality of the spiritual world' (289). For James himself, pressing existential questions and the lingering threat of a personal breakdown were at stake. Accordingly, Schmidt argues, his mysticism is constructed as 'a way to unleash energy [...] to encourage the heroic, the strenuous, and the vital' (292).

The upshot of this analysis is that neither 'religious experience' nor 'mysticism' can be taken for granted. These are constructs with a history rooted in the course of Western Christianity itself, and their development implies an imaginative activism, as in James's frank admission that 'I have grown so out of Christianity that entanglement therewith on the part of a mystical utterance has to be abstracted from and overcome before I can listen' (quoted in Schmidt 2003: 294). There is, then, an ongoing intellectual drama of 'overcoming' for the historian and critic to uncover here. Such a genealogical approach also appears relevant to an account of the threat of nihilism and attendant sense of subjective dissolution, chaos and *anomie* that many Modernists began to discern in the condition of late nineteenth-century modernity.

My approach on this point differs significantly from that of Roger Griffin, who argues that the disturbing sense of a breakdown of meaning in late modernity should be understood in terms of 'archetypal, perennial aspects of human culture': 'Our argument posits an innate human faculty for projecting onto the "brute facts" of external reality an infinite abundance of significant patterns, of symbolic meanings, of ultimate purposes, all rooted in a higher order, whether immanent or supernatural' (Griffin 2007: 73). Thus, when faced with the breakdown of such 'sacred canopies', an 'abyss of meaninglessness' is laid bare: 'The opposite of the sacred is thus not just the profane but, at a deeper level, chaos, the intimation of nothingness' (75). Griffin goes on to invoke the tradition of social psychology known after Ernst Becker as Terror Management Theory in order to explain among other things 'the never-ending proliferation under modernity of strategies for anaesthetizing existential pain' (87), since the encounter with the abyss is humanly intolerable, and the gap must be closed.

One must of course agree that the need for meaning is a fundamental human motivation, and also that the Modernist sense of crisis was often precipitated by a perceived threat of the breakdown of meaning. However, Griffin's move towards the 'archetypal' also conceals the cultural specificity of the whole idea that humanly constructed meanings really are mere 'projections' onto a primordial 'abyss of meaninglessness'. On this point, Griffin is prone to quoting Modernist writers (such as Samuel Beckett (Griffin 2007: 75–6)) *in support* of the idea of a 'primordial angst of the void' (75), even as that idea is being invoked to explain the motivation behind their writings. Whether or not this is wholly circular is less important here: the point is that this procedure forestalls a historical approach to the expression of 'cosmic absurdity' (75) in such writers as Beckett, considered as emerging very much from within the history of Western metaphysics and theology, even in and through a rebellion against that tradition.[23] While Beckett will be the subject of Chapter 4 of this book, our immediate task must be to sketch the theological backdrop to Western nihilism and subjective *anomie*.

First, however, a methodological note. The historical analysis in this study is intended to be 'metaphysically' completely neutral. That is to say, a scholar personally committed (as Griffin seems to be) to what the theologian John Milbank has called an 'ontology of violence'[24] (positing a primordial strife, or chaos, or matter void of human meaning) should nonetheless be able to appreciate the kind of conceptual genealogy presented in the Schmidt article discussed above, simply as a contribution to our knowledge; and likewise for the account of Western nihilism that follows. Correspondingly, a scholar personally committed to an 'ontology of peace' (Being as a divine gift) must of course still acknowledge the insights from social psychology emphasized by Griffin, however much he or she might be inclined to interpret the human search for meaning as ultimately a search for God. Overall, then, one desired outcome of this study would be to promote a fuller conversation between such scholars on the topic of Modernism.

Philosophical nihilism will be approached here through the work of John Milbank and the Radical Orthodoxy school of theologians,[25] whereas the sense of subjective 'dissolution' and *anomie* will be discussed via Charles Taylor's study *A Secular Age* (2007), abetted by insights from Louis A. Sass's book *Madness and Modernism* (1992). Space permits only bare-bones summary of highly selective points, and it bears noting that various details of these scholars' meaty historical narratives have naturally been contested. Yet for our immediate purpose of reconceiving 'Modernism and Christianity' as a field of study, it is the mere fact that 'nihilism' (and modernity) can be theologically genealogized that counts. In some concluding remarks on Nietzsche, I will suggest how that fact can be converted into a certain 'cash value' for the further study of central Modernist figures.

John Milbank's *Theology and Social Theory* is the founding text of the Radical Orthodoxy school. It famously opens, 'Once, there was no "secular"', meaning that 'The secular as a domain had to be instituted or *imagined*, both in theory and in practice' (Milbank 2006: 9). Hence, 'This institution [of the secular] is not correctly grasped in merely negative terms as a desacralization', that is, it did *not* develop simply from 'the removal of the superfluous and additional to leave a residue of the human, the natural and the self-sufficient' (9). Instead, behind the 'positive institution of the secular' as a slow, piecemeal intellectual and cultural product is the specific 'self-understanding of Christianity arrived at in late-medieval nominalism, the Protestant reformation and seventeenth-century Augustinianism, which completely privatized, spiritualized and transcendentalized the sacred, and concurrently reimagined nature, human action and society as a sphere of autonomous, sheerly formal power' (9). This autonomous sphere of power was developed, for instance, in the work of political theorists such as Hugo Grotius and Thomas Hobbes, as 'the new science of politics both assumed and constructed for itself a new autonomous object – the political – defined as a field of pure power' (10). The theological roots of this idea of a self-sufficient, immanent, secular realm go back further still, to the thirteenth-century nominalist conception of the 'univocity of being'. John Duns Scotus placed God and creatures under a *common* concept of 'being', whereas with Thomas Aquinas, God and creatures had been treated as utterly different in kind (there is only *one* self-subsistent Being, God, in which creatures share by analogical participation) (Oliver 2009: 22). The long-term consequence of this shift was that 'God is understood to lie at the far side of an untraversable infinite sea of being', and this 'opens up the possibility of a space for which God is largely irrelevant' (22). This bracketing of God eventually makes conceivable (or constructible) the realm of what Nietzsche would call the 'will-to-power': an end-lessly unfolding strife or chaos, seemingly in motion but ultimately a ceaseless repetition of the same, for 'the univocal process is abso-lutely indifferent to each particular difference' (Milbank 2006: 308). On this reading, nihilism may be understood as the contemplation of that realm or process – an activity that can be frightening and might lead one to seek refuge in sundry redemptive schemes, as many Modernists have done.

However, it will not do to posit philosophical nihilism as the nec-essary and sufficient motivation behind the widespread sense of sub-jective *anomie* that Griffin identifies; for the phenomenon reached far beyond intellectual circles. Charles Taylor's *A Secular Age* develops a genealogy of the secular that is complementary to that of the Milbank school,[26] focusing upon the gradual transition from what he calls the 'porous self' of premodern times to the 'buffered self' of modernity. In the 'enchanted' premodern world 'the porous self is vulnerable, to spirits, demons, cosmic forces' and in general, the 'boundary between mind and world is porous' (Taylor 2007: 38–9). Crucially, then,

> living in the enchanted, porous world of our ancestors was inherently liv-ing socially. It was not just that the spiritual forces which impinged on me often emanated from people around me [...] Much more fundamentally, these forces often impinged on us as a society, and were defended against by us as a society. (42)

In turn, this 'puts a tremendous premium on holding on to the con-sensus', since 'the deviancy of some would call down punishment on all' (42). Accordingly, in this world, 'society, this utterly solid and indispensable reality, argues for God. Not only does it follow: I have moral and spiritual aspirations, therefore God is; but also: we are linked in society, therefore God is' (43). By contrast, the 'buffered' self involves 'a world in which the only locus of thoughts, feelings, spiritual élan is what we call minds; the only minds in the cosmos are those of humans [...] and minds are bounded, so that these thoughts, feelings, etc., are situated "within" them' (30). Given this 'thick emotional boundary between us and the cosmos' (38), the possibility always exists of 'disengaging from everything outside the mind. My ultimate purposes are those which arise within me, the cru-cial meanings of things are those defined in my responses to them' (38). 'Connected to our firm placing of the non-human world outside

the mind', furthermore, 'is our perception of it as exceptionless natural law' (40). In the enchanted world, rejecting God therefore meant
'chancing ourselves in the field of forces without him' (41), abandoning His protection, but with disenchantment, this rejection can be
figured as 'retiring to the safe redoubt of the buffered self' (41). Taylor's
776-page account is gradualist and multi-factored, but he is especially
insightful on how the very possibility of anything like an exclusive
Western humanism could only emerge 'out of earlier Christian forms'
(28), utilizing a *moral* impetus rooted in the buffered self: '[Human-
ism] had to include the active capacity to shape and fashion our
world, natural and social; and it had to be actuated by some drive to
human beneficence', some 'substitute for agape' (27). Thus, the transition from porous to buffered self could be positively constructed
as an escape from an unnecessary fear of things 'outside', and as an
opportunity for this self to be 'giving its own autonomous order to its
life', in order to achieve 'self-control or self-direction' (38–9).

Nevertheless, this transition also involves a potential sense of 'loss'
(Taylor 2007: 38), in the felt disconnect between self and world, and
in the increasing dissociation of the individual from a society that
is no longer inherently linked to the divine. Roger Griffin's list of
the socially atomizing, disorientating processes of late nineteenth-
century modernity springs to mind here (see p. 2). Indeed, Taylor's
approach is perhaps too gradualist to really capture the specifically
Modernist crisis of the buffered self. A more apt diagnosis may, I pro-
pose, be found by adopting Louis Sass's suggestive linkage of the
'hyper-reflexive' self of schizophrenia with the wider Modernist crisis
of subjectivity.

According to Sass, three characteristic modes of 'hyper-reflexivity'
found in both schizophrenia and Modernism are particularly relevant in approaching the Modernist crisis of self. The first mode is
'perspectivism and relativism' (Sass 1992: 30), indicating the post-
Kantian emphasis upon the observer's creative role in perception.
This is exemplified in artworks that insist on the limitations of any
single perspective, *or* in those that systematically multiply perspectives: 'Impressionist paintings and novels such as Virginia Woolf's
Mrs Dalloway might exemplify the first sort; analytic cubist paintings and novels such as William Faulkner's *The Sound and the Fury*
and Woolf's *The Waves* illustrate the second' (31). Correspondingly, this
sense of the world as, in Nietzsche's words, 'a perspectival appearance
whose origin lies in us' (quoted in Sass 1992: 31) is related to two kinds

of potential psychic breakdown. For Sass, these are but two sides of the same coin: *either* the 'vertiginous sense of power inherent in seeing reality as a figment of one's own, all-powerful self' – *or* 'a despairing recognition of the ultimate meaninglessness and absurdity of the human world' (31).

The second mode Sass calls 'dehumanization', meaning 'a loss of the self's sense of unity and of its capacity for effective or voluntary action' (Sass 1992: 31). Again this has two sides. The self might come to seem a 'mere occasion for the swarming of independent subjective events' ('common in novels by Ford Madox Ford, Virginia Woolf, and Nathalie Sarraute' (31)), and this can fragment and obliterate the sense of unity and control (31). Contrariwise, there is an 'extreme kind of objectivism'; one whereby, equally paralysingly, 'human activity is observed with the coldest and most external of gazes' (31), as in Wyndham Lewis's aesthetic of 'deadness'.

The third mode focuses on world more than self. On the one hand, in many Modernist works and in some schizophrenic states, 'the world seems to be *derealized*, robbed of its substantiality or objectivity, its ontological status as an entity or horizon independent of the perceiving subject' (Sass 1992: 32). 'In the poet Stéphane Mallarmé's influential ideal of a literature of absence we find the literary equivalent', continues Sass, 'a poetry preoccupied with its own sounds and syntax, seeking to negate rather than to evoke a realm of external objects and events' (32). On the other hand, external reality can seem to lose 'not its substantiality and otherness but its human resonance or significance' (33), as with the novelist Alain Robbe-Grillet's *chosisme*, a world of things that 'simply *is*' (33).

 At the root of all these symptoms, then, is the 'hyper-conscious' experience of the self, not as embedded in ordinary, practical, social activity, but primarily *as* 'subject'; namely, the being 'for whom and by whom the world is represented' (Sass 1992: 33). Clearly, Taylor's account of the buffered self, capable of 'disengaging from everything outside the mind' (Taylor 2007: 38), effectively provides the cultural genealogy of the very condition so aptly described by Sass. Although such disengagement *need* not precipitate any schizophrenic breakdown, the threat of such symptoms does clearly affect Modernist art and thought.

The topic of 'genealogies' in relation to Modernism and Christianity inevitably recalls Nietzsche's *On the Genealogy of Morals* (1887), and the promised 'cash value' for Modernist studies of the theological genealogies of Western modernity sketched here via Milbank and Taylor may now be extracted in relation to that influential work. Put simply, it considerably sharpens our critical sense of the specificity and imaginative activism of Nietzsche's genealogy of Christian morality and metaphysics if his approach is measured against a fuller account of the very theological themes he is trying to subvert. Once again, this is so regardless of whether one is finally in sympathy with his analysis or not.

Only the barest indication of such a procedure can be offered here, with the help of the theologian David Bentley Hart's self-consciously oppositional Nietzsche reading (which draws on Milbank's 'ontology of peace/violence' distinction).[27] It will be recalled that Nietzsche's fundamental question in the *Genealogy* was,

> under what conditions did man invent the value-judgements good and evil? *And what value do they themselves possess?* Have they helped or hindered the progress of mankind? Are they a sign of indigence, of impoverishment, of the degeneration of life? Or do they rather reveal the plenitude, the strength, the will of life, its courage, confidence, and future?
>
> (Nietzsche 2008: 5)

Whereas for Nietzsche, 'good and *bad*' is a distinction that derives from the self-assertion of the noble masters who could affirm their own positive qualities (power, superiority, refinement), 'good and *evil*' derives from 'slave morality', famously mocked in the following terms:

> The miserable alone are good; the poor, the powerless, the low alone are the good. The suffering, the deprived, the sick, the ugly are the only pious ones, the only blessed, for them alone is there salvation. You, on the other hand, the noble and the powerful, you are for all eternity the evil, the cruel, the lascivious, the insatiable, the godless ones. (19)

Accordingly, Christian 'love' is a concealed form of hatred, 'the kind of hatred which creates ideals and changes the meaning of values, a hatred the like of which has never been on earth', while the 'triumphant crown' of that hatred was 'Jesus of Nazareth, as the gospel of love incarnate, this "redeemer" bringing victory to the poor, the sick, the sinners' (20).

For David Bentley Hart, Christian theology can 'glimpse something of its own depths in the mirror of [Nietzsche's] contempt' (Hart

2004: 94), for 'Christianity did indeed subvert the language of noble virtue, especially insofar as the latter presupposed the necessity of strife and honoured strength for its own sake; Christianity, in its origins, perversely refrained from the celebration of acquisition and dominion' (116). The astonishing novelty of Christianity is thus 'irreconcilably subversive of all the values of antique virtue and public philosophy' (123):

> Christians claim that the beauty that appears in Christ, contrary to all judicious taste, abides with and in the poor, the godforsaken, the forgotten, and the lowly, not simply as a sweetening of their lot with bootless sentimentality, or because Christianity cherishes life only when it is weak, perishing, and uncomely, but because Christ – who is the truth of being – in dwelling among and embracing these 'slaves', shows them to be luminously beautiful. (123–4)

This then is the vision that Nietzsche set out to overcome, but he would be the first to admit its power and allure. As scholars of Modernism, we should do no less.

Conclusion: Tracing Christianity in Modernism

Nietzsche would also be the first to admit that to proclaim the death of God is no neutral observation of fact: it is attempted murder. Extending this insight, for the purposes of Modernism and Christianity studies, the idea of 'secularization' should certainly not be understood as a process somehow over and done with by the year 1900, but as marking an ongoing battle zone well into the twentieth century. One important component of this claim would be recent work by scholars who have significantly nuanced the remarkably ingrained picture of a Christianity supposedly wholly spent as a cultural force by the turn of the twentieth century. Timothy Larsen has argued that alongside the 'crisis of faith' in nineteenth-century Britain there was also a significant 'crisis of doubt', whereby a number of one-time secularists (and some rank and file along with them) re-converted to Christian faith; this was a two-way process all along (Larsen 2008). The continuing appeal of faith into the twentieth century is attested in such studies as Patrick Allitt's *Catholic Converts: British and American Intellectuals Turn to Rome* (1997) and Stephen Schloesser's *Jazz Age Catholicism: Mystic Modernism in Postwar Paris 1919–1933* (2005), the latter of which is encountered in the next chapter. Peter J. Bowler, in *Reconciling Science and Religion: The Debate in Early Twentieth-Century Britain* (2001), has similarly shown that this debate was far from over by 1900. On the contrary, it was very much in keeping with the times for scientists, philosophers and sundry cultural figures to hold religious and often specifically Christian views. More expansively, Brian Sudlow offers a good overview of the blend of issues of sociology, policy and ideology that may be quoted as indicators of 'secularization' in both France and England between 1880 and 1914 (Sudlow 2011). However, his headings (in ch. 1) should be read precisely as the demarcation of skirmishes in an unfolding battle in which any neutrality was very hard to maintain: 'positivism and scientism'; 'deism and anticlericalism'; 'irreligious anti-materialism'; 'utilitarianism'; 'progress as ideology'; 'anthropology and proto-relativism'; 'religious doubt and hostility'; 'marriage and divorce'; 'the separation of Church and State' (in France); 'the secularization of the school system' (France); 'the expulsion of religious congregations' (France); 'blasphemy' (England); 'state religion, disabilities, and oaths' (England) – these all point up still *unresolved* tensions. It is also worth remarking here that both secularists and Christians at this time could and did invoke the idea of a process of secularization as a rhetorical ploy in itself: the former to argue that it was already unstoppable or needed to be completed, and the latter to argue that it should be reversed.

We have seen in this chapter that the early Modernist period was rife with an immense variety of religious or *ersatz* religious impulses, manifesting themselves across a range of cultural and sociopolitical areas. Furthermore, it has been argued that given the fundamental theme of an epochal transformation within Modernism, the cultural force and historical role of Christianity simply could not be overlooked by Modernists, at least in the vast majority of cases. Moreover, the very idea of 'the secular', and the very condition of modernity, are inextricably involved with the history of Western Christianity itself: a fact that should have wide-ranging consequences for how scholars contextualize Modernist work, thought and activism.

So far, this narrative has focused less on individuals, but it is worth noting at this point that all the six authors treated in the case studies that follow had some form of Christian upbringing: Irish Catholicism for James Joyce; Low Church Anglicanism for David Jones; Unitarianism for T. S. Eliot; Presbyterianism for Ezra Pound; High Church Anglicanism for W. H. Auden; and the Church of Ireland for Samuel Beckett. That they were all fundamentally marked by their backgrounds goes without saying, and the chapters that follow will approach these individuals as highly sensitive conducting-rods for the tensions inherent in the broader field of 'Modernism and Christianity'. Chapter 2 examines the idea of 'Catholic Modernisms' in relation to Joyce and Jones, testing both sides of that equation, 'Catholic' and 'Modernist', against the ideological commitments, creative inspiration and cultural backgrounds of these writers, and arguing that theories of Modernism need to come to terms with this idea. Chapter 3 then discusses the revived interest in Christian dogma as a response to the perceived crisis of civilization in the 1920s and 1930s, persisting into the Second World War: 'Hell' for T. S. Eliot, 'Usury' for Ezra Pound and 'Incarnation' for W. H. Auden. This 'return' to dogma was – in line with the perspective outlined in the present chapter – no mere nostalgia, but a focal point for the creative energies and cultural and political activism of these three writers in their efforts to regenerate and revitalize Western civilization. This penultimate chapter concludes with a discussion of the relationship between dogma, propaganda and poetry in these writers, arguing that Modernism should also be characterized as a 'crisis of authority'. Chapter 4 charts Samuel Beckett's lifelong *agon* with Christianity across four areas that were also central to other Modernist writers: theodicy, the response to Dante and to mysticism, and Beckett's revision of the rhetoric of Apocalypse. Strikingly, Beckett's implicit position is that the 'redemptive' urge within Modernism itself ultimately amounts to watered-down Christianity. His own relentless confrontation with Christianity, focused around the problem of suffering and involving an unending, self-imposed ethical discipline of 'fidelity to failure', is crucial to understanding his aesthetics. Finally, the Conclusion of this book reviews the potential of 'Modernism and Christianity' as a field of studies, arguing that its reach should extend far beyond the parameters of the present contribution.

2

CATHOLIC MODERNISMS: JAMES JOYCE AND DAVID JONES

The phrase 'Catholic Modernisms' should give the reader pause. The Catholic Church at the beginning of the twentieth century waged a very public campaign against theological 'modernism', defined in Pope Pius X's 1907 encyclical *Pascendi Dominici Gregis* as agnosticism regarding knowledge of God (devaluing revelation, scripture and dogma), and as 'vital immanence' – the association of God, not primarily with a pre-existing supernatural order, but with a human desire for the divine that can attach itself to various symbolic forms as it evolves through time. What, if anything, does the battle over theological modernism have to do with the cultural Modernism (capitalized throughout this study) of a novelist such as James Joyce, or a poet and painter such as David Jones?[28] Furthermore, if Joyce, in his own words, 'left the Catholic Church, hating it most fervently', proceeding to 'make open war upon it by what I write and say and do',[29] is it not (as Geert Lernout has recently argued) pointless for the critic to somehow drag this determined anti-Catholic back into the fold by labelling him a 'Catholic' Modernist? Contrariwise, how could Jones – a Catholic convert whose faith was undeniably central to his aesthetics, to his painting and to the palimpsestic poetry of *In Parenthesis* (1937) and *The Anathemata* (1952) – choose to associate himself both with a Church so apparently hostile to all 'modernism', on the one hand, and with cultural-Modernist artistic influences such as Joyce himself, on the other? More generally, is there any theoretical justification in the first place for lumping two artists with such opposing

25

ideologies together as 'cultural Modernists', let alone aligning them as 'Catholic Modernists'? Or, reversing the question, can existing theories of cultural Modernism even account for distinctively 'Catholic Modernisms', and if so, how?

In general, of course, Joyce and Jones are artists whose formally experimental work identifies them as paradigmatic cultural Modernists, however this term is defined, and their thought and work is also indelibly marked by their close encounters with the Roman Catholic Church. Thus the phrase 'Catholic Modernism' here points, for now heuristically, to this conjunction. The next section will relate the respective Catholic Modernisms of Joyce and Jones to the historical context and wider significance of the Vatican's 'war on modernism', but also to other cultural meanings of Catholicism beyond this influential dogmatic dispute. Then, the idea of 'Catholic Modernism' will be examined in light of two established theories of cultural Modernism, that of Toril Moi in *Henrik Ibsen and the Birth of Modernism* (2006), and that of Roger Griffin in *Modernism and Fascism* (2007). Unsurprisingly in view of Joyce's admiration for Ibsen, Moi's view that Modernism 'is built on the negation of idealism' (Moi 2006: 67) fits Joyce most comfortably; whereas Griffin's emphasis upon Modernism as a revolt against a decadent, moribund nineteenth-century modernity matches Jones's case better. Both models, however, are in need of supplementation and refinement when confronted with the Catholic Modernisms of our two authors. The following section applies lessons from this discussion to a comparison of the interlocking themes of Eucharist and artistic creativity in Joyce's *Ulysses* (1922) and Jones's *In Parenthesis* (1937). The conclusion examines Jones's idiosyncratic reading of Joyce's work, drawing from this some methodological implications for further scholarship on 'Catholic Modernisms'.

'Catholic' Modernists?

In an important article, Finn Fordham has shown that the so-called 'modernist controversy' within the Catholic Church was anything but a marginal phenomenon in the public sphere:

> Between 1907 and 1930 there were over 350 references to the term in *The Times*: ninety per cent of these refer to the theological context of modernism; the remainder feature in articles on architecture, music, or

literature. The word 'modernism' in this period could hardly be used without some echo of this other sense.

(Fordham forthcoming)

Fordham points out that the Church's very labelling of a diverse set of intellectuals and groups as 'modernist' – attributing to them a 'synthesis of all heresies' – was part of a strategy of containment:

> Unified by this term, the 'modernists' did not themselves exist as a group: individually they were focused on quite different aims, all hoping though that the Church might evolve its dogma or structures so as to come into harmony with diverse progressive ideas. These included evolution, historicized textuality, hermeneutic indeterminacy, socialism, secularism, communism, feminism, and immanentism: ideas emerging at that time from various academic disciplines or discursive fields, such as philology and philosophy, social and political science, biology and zoology, and also of course theology.

(forthcoming)

Fordham argues that this strategy, while internally successful in the sense that the 'Oath against Modernism' (obligatory for all clergy from 1910) and a systematic campaign against suspected 'modernists' really did suppress these tendencies within the Church by the 1920s, also had an opposite effect in the wider cultural field. The anti-modernism of the Church became a rallying point for a range of opposing tendencies that did not always have much more in common than this resistance itself:

> Following a period in which the Church expressed intense hostility to the idea that dogma might evolve and also sought to shore up the absolute sense of its own absolute permanence, the cultural field produced a string of manifestos that acknowledged the contingencies of history and the ephemerality of cultural forms.

(forthcoming)

Liberalism and individualism in politics and the emphasis on subjectivity and interiority in art and literature could also be associated on this basis. Furthermore, some of the intellectual genealogies produced for what the Vatican called 'modernism' were also, as Fordham shows via this quotation from a review by Dean William Inge of Maud Petre's *Modernism: Its Failure and Its Fruits* (1918), strikingly close to those one might now adduce for cultural Modernism: 'It would require an essay to trace its affinities with subjective idealism, with post-Kantian relativism, with French fidéisme, with American pragmatism, and with the philosophy of Bergson.'[30] In a broader survey of nineteenth-century uses of the term 'modernism', Fordham also finds a persistent association of this term with modern irreligion, for instance in John Ruskin's opposition of the religious art of the medieval period to a decadently profane 'modernism' characterizing both the era and its art. After *Pascendi Gregis*, the avant-garde journal *The New Age* could respond with a reversal of this dichotomy, predicting the onset of 'the final battle between the medieval and modern methods of thought'.[31] The scene was set for 'an eventual counter-appropriation of the term as a positive sign' (Fordham forthcoming) in the cultural field.

Fordham's argument captures one crucial strain within the historical formation of cultural Modernism, namely the uniting of quite disparate (even contradictory)[32] trends by a common and prominent enemy in Catholic anti-modernism. Yet his emphasis on the contrast between a 'reactionary' Church and 'progressive liberal individuals' also needs supplementation here. In isolation, this contrast might seem to imply that to qualify as a cultural Modernist *at all*, one needs as it were to play for the latter team against the former. While Fordham takes care to guard against that implication in his conclusion, he does not fully develop another kind of influence of the Catholic Church upon cultural Modernism: its attractiveness. Most familiar here is the emphasis on the aesthetic riches and excess of the Church – its ritual, its costume, its semi-erotic mysticism, its fascination with fallenness and abjection, its baroque scriptures, its opulently suffering Christ – that is associated with *fin de siècle* decadence and symbolism. As Ellis Hanson argues in *Decadence and Catholicism*, this kind of attraction went well beyond dogmatic disputes:

> Catholicism is itself an elaborate paradox. The decadents merely emphasized the point within their own aesthetic of paradox. The Church is at once modern and yet medieval, ascetic and yet sumptuous, spiritual and yet sensual, chaste and yet erotic, homophobic and yet homoerotic, suspicious of aestheticism and yet an elaborate work of art.
>
> (Hanson 1997: 7)

Somewhat less well known, but more immediately relevant here due to its impact on David Jones, is the *renouveau catholique* described in Stephen Schloesser's *Jazz Age Catholicism: Mystic Modernism in Postwar Paris 1919–1933*. In a post-war France traumatized by conflict there arose a marked need for a fresh cultural synthesis that could preserve and reinvigorate religious tradition without shunning artistic confrontation with disruptive experience itself. The movement was fuelled by lay writers and artists like the philosopher Jacques Maritain, the painter Georges Rouault, the novelist Georges Bernanos and the musician Charles Tournemire. At its base was a 'skilful retooling' (Schloesser 2005: 6) of traditional Catholic ideas such as hylomorphism (Aristotelian interrelation of matter and form), sacramentalism (the capability of created things to act as efficacious signs of the work of a transcendent Creator) and transubstantiation (bread and wine becoming Body and Blood in substance, accidents remaining). The result of applying these conceptual resources creatively to the cultural field was a 'dialectical realism' that could respond subtly to modern experience while sidestepping the sharp divide between ultramontanist orthodoxy and 'modernist' heresy:

> For modernists and ultramontanist Catholics alike, the dominant cultural realism (e.g., positivism and historicism; literary grotesqueries; pictorial prostitutes, beggars and clowns; musical chromaticism, passions, and dissonance) had seemed incompatible with a religion defined in opposition to those elements. [. . .] However, by recovering and recasting its dialectical tradition – in other words, through using the Church's own heritage – Catholic revivalists could re-imagine the relationship between religion and culture. Catholicism and 'modern civilization' – eternal and avantgarde, grace and grotesque, mystical and dissonant – could now be seen in categories other than simple competition: form actualizing matter, grace perfecting nature, substance underlying surface.
>
> (Schloesser 2005: 7)

Maritain, the movement's chief ideologue who would also be a fundamental influence on David Jones, used Thomist philosophy to define the task of modern art in his *Art et scholastique* (1920). Its central strategic distinction is between the virtues of Prudence and Art. Prudence is connected with the order of Doing: it is the domain of 'Morality, or the good man as such'; it is the guide to practical action (Maritain 1923: 7). Art, by contrast, is always a kind of Making, 'ordered to such and such a particular end, taken in itself and self-sufficing, not to the common end of human life, and it is related to the proper good or perfection, not of the man who works, but of the work effected' (8). Simply put, a 'good' craftsman makes a good chair, and his personal morality is here irrelevant. In fact, Art 'settles the *artifex*, artist or craftsman, in a world apart, fenced, bounded, detached, where it puts man's strength and man's intelligence and man's time at the service of a thing which he is making' (8) Art is thus autonomous: this for Maritain avoided the submission of Art to mere nineteenth-century *bien pensant* respectability, and ensured that Art could take anything (even the ugly or the discordant) as material for its making.[33] On the other hand, the high value placed on human craftsmanship also implied a fierce critique of a modern technocratic, industrial and utilitarian civilization that had just emerged from a war that seemed to treat human beings as mere raw material. Both the modern battlefield and the modern factory degraded the natural condition of man as *artifex* to something inhuman or subhuman. Accordingly, Catholic theology now seemed to affirm artistic autonomy and the full breadth of artistic responses to modern experience ('dialectical realism'), while also offering a vision of the healing and re-integration of a culture that seemed hostile to authentic human making and creativity.

After this preamble, we can begin to place Joyce and Jones in this cultural landscape. As Fordham points out, and as Geert Lernout has documented in great detail, Joyce took a conscious, consistent and well-informed stand against ultramontanist anti-Modernism – his hostility going well beyond those of theological 'modernists' (who after all still desired to stay within the Church) – to the point where he could declare with Stephen Dedalus that 'You behold in me a horrible example of free thought' (JJU, 20). Joyce's Jesuit schooling at Clongowes Wood and later at Belvedere College familiarized him at an early age with the doctrine and liturgy and culture of a militantly orthodox Irish Catholicism recently reformed in an ultramontane direction (see Lernout 2010: 42). He was an earnest believer at one time, a Prefect of his Sodality and marked out for the priesthood. To judge by the semi-autobiographical *A Portrait of the Artist as a Young Man* (1914–15), all this appealed to his sense of pride in being singled out from among his peers. However, *Portrait* also indicates that his intense immersion in the faith also seems to have become oppressive to the young Joyce: the vivid threat of Hell alternating with Marian devotions that conveyed an exalted but ultimately cloying purity. The issue of sexual purity especially would precipitate revolt, and the sense that his 'nature', and indeed human nature, was cruelly denied by the Church would become a lifelong theme: 'I am nauseated by the lying drivel about pure men and pure women and spiritual love and love for ever: blatant lying in the face of the truth'.[34] If his letter to his partner Nora Barnacle (29 August 1904) quoted before[35] is accurate, he effectively left the Church at about age 16 and started a 'secret war' on it that would become an open one by the time he left the Royal University (now University College Dublin). The same letter states that he 'declined to accept the positions' that Catholicism offered him, and Lernout's book amply testifies to this. He lived with Nora outside marriage, away from Irish propriety on the continent; he did not have his children baptized, expressly aiming to deprive the Church of members; whilst living in Catholic Pola and later in Rome his letters are full of harsh anti-clerical outbursts, coupled with anarchic-socialist politics; his brother's diary suggests that he was at one time attracted to Nietzschean philosophy, proclaiming 'all kinds of anti-Christian ideals – selfishness, licentiousness, pitilessness';[36] and Lernout details his copious study of modern atheist or agnostic 'freethinkers' on the one hand, and the whole history of heresy, schism and dissent within Christianity on the other (Lernout 2010: ch. 3). Joyce thus structured his private life partly in objection to the Church ('How I hate God and death! How I like Nora!'),[37] while cultivating a public intellectual disdain for its teaching. Even a freethinker such as the biblical critic Ernest Renan displayed too much 'regret at having to abandon dear old Grandmother Church'[38] for his taste.

Joyce is of course not just any Modernist: his iconic status and direct influence upon a host of other writers is surely central to the historical appropriation of an ideologically anti-Catholic 'Modernism' as a positive sign described by Fordham. The *frisson* of being a heretical, banned and attacked writer – cultivated by Joyce himself – combined with praise from the intelligentsia, and the inventiveness of the work itself, to create a perfect storm of notoriety. But given his views and cultural positioning, why call him a 'Catholic' Modernist at all?

Geert Lernout's book intervenes in a long debate within Joyce studies on whether Joyce's 'mind' in some sense remained indelibly Catholic despite his protestations to the contrary. Lernout's case that this notion does not stand up to scrutiny is overwhelming. However, this does not alter the fact that Joyce's aesthetics and literary works would be simply unimaginable, in all their specificity, without the ingredient of Catholicism. Joyce remained resolutely anti-Catholic in his views, but he may still be called a 'Catholic Modernist', as opposed to those cultural Modernists who were not specially influenced by the Catholic Church. This perspective allows us to see that his *agon* with Catholicism is a source of creative energy in his work: for instance, in fuelling its parodical vigour. Another useful suggestion here comes from Joyce's acquaintance Louis Gillet: Irish politics were too parochial to offer a grand canvas for Joyce, but 'to declare war on heaven meant stepping out of local intrigues; it meant giving to this enterprise a titanic character and placing oneself on the level with the universe' (quoted in Lernout 2010: 109). Furthermore, it should also be acknowledged that Joyce (like the *fin de siècle* writers in this one respect at least) did retain a fascination with the aesthetics of rite and liturgy. Lernout mentions the well-known story about how Joyce in Trieste would attend the Paschaltide liturgy, 'in which he identified so much with the fate of Jesus that he would have tears in his eyes' (2010: 109), but he does not comment on how this attraction affected Joyce's literary art, a subject we will return to when dealing with *Ulysses* below.

Another kind of paradoxical attraction of the Church for Joyce is also well known, and overlaps to some degree with Maritain's aesthetic Thomism. In *A Portrait of the Artist*, Stephen's famous definition of the artist's relationship to his work evokes the distinction between Art and Prudence, and recalls Aquinas's view that 'The goodness of a work of art is to be judged not in terms of the artist, but rather in terms of the art-work itself.'[39] 'The artist, like the God of the creation, remains within or behind or beyond or above his handiwork, invisible, refined out of existence, indifferent, paring his fingernails' (JJPA, 181). As William T. Noon has pointed out, however, Joyce's emphasis on the autonomy of the work of art (scoffing at the 'antique principle that the end of art is to instruct, to elevate, and to amuse' (JJSH, 79)) is distinctly modern and foreign to Aquinas (Noon 1957: 30). The philosopher acknowledges no category of the 'fine arts' or the 'aesthetic' as a separate realm ('for the most part he talks about such "arts" as farming, medicine, or preaching' (32)); and he is also clear that if any art is used for an evil end it can legitimately be 'stamped out by the civil power' (31). In fact, the parodic intent of Joyce's passage is evident in the irreverent analogy between Creator and artist, 'paring his fingernails'. Part of the point of Stephen's aesthetic theory is to turn the Church's own Angelic Doctor against the moralistic and 'Puritanic' (JJSH, 79) contemporary Irish Church. As Dominic Mangianello has shown, Stephen's theory of aesthetic impersonality has clear political implications in that the aim is to 'expose narrow ideals of life through his art' (Mangianello 1980: 42). Furthermore,

Stephen's acceptance of the artistic vocation as opposed to holy orders [...] is an act replete with political connotations. The priest as 'natural leader' of his flock holds sway not only in spiritual matters but also in Irish temporal affairs. The director who makes Stephen the offer describes the 'awful power' invested in the priesthood: 'No king or emperor on this earth has the power of the priest of God'.

(Mangianello 1980: 39; JJPA, 133)

Stephen in fact appropriates this power for his artistic vocation, while denigrating the priesthood itself, here in a brooding fit over the unattainable Emma: 'To [the priest] she would unveil her soul's shy nakedness, to one who was but schooled in the discharging of a formal rite rather than to him, a priest of the eternal imagination, transmuting the daily bread of experience into the radiant body of everliving life' (JJPA, 186). Central to this 'transmutation' is the experience of 'epiphany', which is associated (quite explicitly in *Stephen Hero*, the first draft towards *Portrait*) with the third of Aquinas's requirements for beauty, *claritas* or radiance:

First we recognise that the object is *one* integral thing, then we recognise that it is an organised composite structure, a *thing* in fact: finally, when the relation of the parts is exquisite, when the parts are adjusted to the special point, we recognise that it is *that* thing which it is. Its soul, its whatness, leaps to us from the vestment of its appearance. The soul of the commonest object, the structure of which is so adjusted, seems to us radiant. The object achieves its epiphany.

(JJSH, 213)

The 'daily bread of experience' and 'the commonest object' – the ordinary, material world – remains the real focus for Joyce, but as Noon points out, in Aquinas the issue is trinitarian theology. There, *claritas* involves a certain 'blaze of being' (Noon 1957: 26), and the beauty in question is, Noon says, one 'which the eye has not seen, nor the ear heard' (26). Joyce's appropriation of Aquinas once again deliberately reverses the priorities: matter trumps transcendence. Yet the utility of Catholic imagery for Joyce goes beyond this level of aggressive protest: for, when examining *Ulysses* below, we shall see how the determined transmutation of Catholic imagery into a materialist and realist artistic vision also serves to endow that vision itself with an aura of redemption. Joyce needs Catholicism not just as a Grand

Enemy, but also as a vital quarry for images that can infuse some measure of 'epiphanic' transcendence into his artistic fascination with the ordinary.

In the case of David Jones, the 'Catholic' designation is straightforward and uncontested, in so far as he remained, as he often put it, 'of Catholic subscription' (DJEA, 109) from his conversion and reception into the Church in 1921 until his death in 1974. However, there is a distinct generational shift between Jones and Joyce, and a very different set of cultural experiences and influences are at play in his development.[40] Jones's father James was a Low Church lay preacher of Welsh extraction. Jones grew up in London but identified just as strongly with his Welsh roots. The son's conversion would be painful to the father, and the ambiguous interrelations between Catholicism, Englishness and Welshness would become a permanent theme for Jones. From very early childhood, Jones's extraordinary artistic talent was evident, and his parents eventually allowed him from the age of 14 to attend the Camberwell School of Arts and Crafts: Jones's sense of an artistic vocation was by the end of his time there so strong that he refused to sit for an art teacher's examination and expected to forego marriage due to his commitment to the unremunerative fine arts (Dilworth 2012: 31). At this point, war broke out, and a defining feature of Jones's experience as a young man would be his participation as a private soldier in the Royal Welch Fusiliers during the Great War of 1914–18. He was wounded at Mametz Wood but survived the war with only psychological damage, though he would later undergo therapy for various nervous breakdowns in part connected with his experiences. The inhumane technologies of this war – machine guns, poison gas – impressed on him a sense of a thoroughgoing civilizational break; the unprecedented diminishment and dispatch of so many individual lives contrasted sharply with the camaraderie of soldiering itself, which Jones tended to associate with heroic and chivalric models from the past. In 1917, he came across a Catholic Mass in progress, quite close to the front line. Gazing surreptitiously, he sensed a deep bond between the priest and these burly men, and the whole scene became for him an epiphanic vision of peace somehow transcending the 'panorama of desolation' (Dilworth 2012: 152). After his discharge in 1919 he began studying at the Westminster School of Art. Two lasting influences from these years would be his reading of Post-Impressionist art theory, and his encounter with Father John O'Connor, the translator of Jacques Maritain's *Art et scholastique*, who began to introduce Jones to Maritain's thought. Through Father O'Connor, Jones also met the sculptor Eric Gill in January 1921 at Ditchling Common. Jones would become part of Gill's artistic community at Ditchling and later at Capel-y-ffin in Wales for the next seven years. Gill was a Catholic, but hardly a conventional one. His fraternity, the 'Guild of SS Joseph and Dominic', practised simple living and emulated medieval hands-on craftsmanship, disdaining modern industrial capitalism and its factories (William Morris's socialism was an important early influence on Gill). In August 1921, after some months of immersion into this community and its fervent discussion of art – centring on Maritain – Jones was received into the Catholic Church by Father O'Connor.

Jones encountered Maritain's philosophy of art at a time when he was experiencing a crisis of vocation as an artist, and this influence would form the spine of all his subsequent artistic theorizing and practice. Crucial here was Maritain's distinction between the virtues of Art and Prudence, and the delineation of the self-sufficiency and universality of the realm of Making as aimed only at the proper good of the thing made. The idea of the *artifex* dedicating himself to a near-ascetic service to the perfection of the thing made was part of the attraction of the Gill group for Jones. At the same time, Maritain seemed to offer a bridge between the special vocation of the artist and a compelling account of human nature. Jones later recalled that he had found one 'key' to his thinking in Post-Impressionist theory, which famously, in Roger Fry's words, had argued that these artists 'do not seek to imitate form, but to create form; not to imitate life, but to find an equivalent for life', to be sought in a 'purely abstract language of form – a visual music'.[41] But on Jones's reading the issue went far beyond a single school of painting, for what held *any* work of human art together was a certain 'abstract *quality*', a 'juxtaposing of forms' without which 'a "thing" having integration and a life of its own, could not be. Therefore without it the arts could not be' (DJDG, 42–3). This generalization springs from Maritain's definition of Art in general as 'intellectual in category, its action consists in impressing an idea upon a material: therefore it resides in the understanding of the *artifex*' as 'a certain *quality* of this understanding' (Maritain 1923: 10) materially externalized. Man as such for Jones is thus an artist, whose form-making is sharply distinguished from the strictly utilitarian making of the animals by containing an element of the gratuitous, and by involving *signs*:

> If we could catch the beaver placing never so small a twig *gratuitously* we could make his dam into a font, he would be patient of baptism — the whole 'sign-world' would be open to him, he would know 'sacrament' and would have a true culture, for a culture is nothing but a sign, and the *anathemata* of a culture, the 'things set up', can only be set up to the gods.
>
> (DJEA, 88)

Jones's way into Catholic theology, and his deep appreciation of the Church's liturgical practice, is entirely based around this understanding of 'man as artist'. But 'sacrament' also became for Jones a term that to some extent floated free of Catholic liturgy or dogma. In his most extensive summary of his long-standing views, the essay 'Art and Sacrament' from 1955, he argued that 'man is unavoidably a sacramentalist and that his works are sacramental in character'; this included Paleolithic man, who 'juxtaposed marks on surfaces not with merely utile, but with significant, intent; that is to say a "re-presenting", a "showing again under other forms", an "effective recalling" of something was intended' (DJEA, 155). Sign-making is here sacramental in its very nature, an implicitly religious act, a 'setting up' to the gods.

But what, then, of Church sacraments? Jones was fond of quoting the French theologian Maurice de la Taille on how Christ, in offering himself in the Eucharist, 'placed Himself in the order of signs' (de la Taille 1934: 211; DJEA, 179). When man is seen as essentially man-the-artist and a sign-maker, Christ's humanity becomes tied to his 'being man-the-artist along with us' (DJEA 167); he thus both assumes and dignifies that humanity. De la Taille argues along traditional lines that the reason why 'Christ in his own person wished to become a sacrament' through his unified action in the Cenacle, upon the Cross, and at Mass, was to establish an 'efficacious sign' recalling the Christian ecclesial body 'united to Christ, aggregated to Christ, incorporated in Christ, one in Christ' (de la Taille 1934: 211). But Jones, going beyond de la Taille, is just as concerned with how Christ's action 'presupposes the sign-world and looks back to foreshadowing rites and arts of mediation and conjugation stretching back for tens of thousands of years in actual pre-history' (DJEA, 167). Indeed, for Jones, Christ's entry into the 'order of signs' seems to imply a kind of consecration, not just of the ecclesial body, but of all human culture.

This perspective may or may not border on the heterodox in terms of Catholic theology[42] but Jones, being an artist not a theologian, was never asked any awkward questions by the institutional Church.

More to the point in our context, this narrative about Jones's background and views indicates that becoming a Catholic was not incidental, but instrumental in turning him into an experimental, Modernist artist. On a personal level, Catholicism enabled him to begin to make sense of his war experiences and to recommit to his artistic vocation; it brought him into an alternative and counter-cultural milieu where he learned new artistic skills, found new direction and started to develop a diagnosis of his times and the place of art in such times. This diagnosis, heavily indebted to Gill and Maritain, emphasized an unprecedented tension between man's essential nature as artist and a technocratic, utilitarian modern civilization capable of industrial warfare on a mass scale. Rejection of the cultural status quo and formal experimentation of course tend to go hand in hand for all Modernists, but Jones's emphasis on the analogy between the 'sacramentalism' of sign-making in general and Catholic sacraments adds a distinctive twist to his work. Both as artist and as poet that work is palimpsestic, endlessly fascinated by dense, half-inaccessible layers of meaning stretching back through past cultures into the pre-history of human sign-making; it is fragmentary, inspecting ruins and traces, juxtaposing past and present through image and word; and it continually pushes the parallels between sign-making and Catholic sacrament to extremes, the one bleeding into the other, in a 'vulnerable',[43] open-ended effort to search for Christ even within the dehumanization and debris of modern culture, 'For it is easy to miss Him / at the turn of a civilization' ('A, a, a, DOMINE DEUS', in Jones 1995: 9).

Extrapolating from this discussion of the 'Catholic' label as applied to both Joyce and Jones, it should not be controversial to call a writer or artist a 'Catholic' cultural Modernist when their engagement with the Catholic Church fuels and permeates their work, thought and aesthetics. It then becomes crucial to establish exactly how that relationship started and developed in individual cases; whether it involves a rejection or an embrace of the Church, and what 'version' of the Church is being constructed in that act; what influences are at work in such construction; how the relationship between the Church and Western modernity, and its role in the development of Western culture, is assessed; and what particular aspects of the Church – dogma, theology, liturgy, customs, art, history, politics, local manifestations – specially engage an individual practitioner. Attention to cultural and historical specificity, and to the ambiguities and complexities of a relationship that can involve simultaneous attraction, rejection and appropriation, is basic to criticism; as is an effort to systematically compare 'Catholic Modernist' case studies. But how does the very idea of a 'Catholic Modernist', as exemplified by Joyce and Jones, fit established theories of cultural Modernism?

Rethinking Cultural Modernism via 'Catholic Modernism'

In the broadest possible terms, as I argued in Chapter 1, to be a cultural Modernist involves responding to Western modernity as having by the late nineteenth century given rise to an unprecedented sense of crisis and epochal transition – a crisis rife with both threat and opportunity, a crisis that must be confronted. Second, it involves shaping one's response (which can be artistic or philosophical, but also political)[44] in a *form* of expression that is itself somehow counter-cultural, experimental and revisionary. Roger Griffin's and Toril Moi's theories of Modernism may be said to emphasize the first and the second of these aspects respectively. The present task is to confront each theory with the respective Catholic Modernisms of Joyce and Jones, to examine whether they are in need of rethinking.

On one level, Griffin's theory matches the case of Jones very well, and helpfully contextualizes a tension that has always been felt in Jones criticism: what Elizabeth Ward calls 'the apparent disjunction between the traditionalist content and the anti-traditionalist form of his poetry' (Ward 1983: 205). By traditionalist content, she means the influence of 'the apocalyptically anti-Renaissance bias traditional in Catholic teaching, based on simultaneous disparagement of the Reformation and celebration of that "great medieval synthesis" which had been given a new lease of life by the Church's deliberate revival of Thomist philosophy in the twentieth century' (58); and also the ideal of 'an organic social existence, ordered, traditional, myth-oriented, but actually defined less in terms of positive attributes than in terms of its dissimilarities from the present' (60). We have seen how Jones (on the same lines as Maritain) understood the modern industrialized, capitalist, 'technocratic', 'megalopolitan'[45] West as hostile to man's essential nature as maker. Ward draws attention to the fact that Jones's Catholic milieu in London in the late 1920s to the early 1930s was distinctly rightist, to the point of envisaging an 'organic revolution', a return to 'the unifying factor from which [the West's] past unity sprang, the Catholic Church' (Ward 1983: 47–8). Jones echoed this revolutionary sentiment from the point of view of his theory of 'man-as-artist', arguing in a 1941 essay called 'Religion and the Muses' that the individual artist in 'our sort of civilization' has become 'a contradiction, a fifth-column, within that civilization, and here it shares the honours of sabotage with the tradition of religion, for both are disruptive forces, both own allegiance to values in any event irritant, and easily becoming toxic to those values which of necessity dominate the present world-orders' (DJEA, 100). This conjunction of 'traditionalism' and 'revolution' is straightforwardly explained by Griffin's framework: what Ward calls 'traditionalism' is in fact being opposed here to a 'decadent' modern civilization, in need of a revitalization cure – through revolution, or at least, for Jones, artistic-religious 'sabotage'. In fact, 'traditionalism' or 'nostalgia' may be misleading labels here, for these 'traditions', should they actually be recovered for the modern world and become dominant, would precisely overturn the cultural status quo. In line with Griffin's observation about fascism (but also other 'conservative revolutionaries'), there is a *futural* dynamic at work here (Griffin 2007: 50, 177–9): or, in Jeffrey Perl's terms, a 'return' for the Modernist does not indicate an (impossible) repetition of the past, but rebirth, re-naissance (Perl 1984: 30–1). In fact, then, there is no logical disjunction between a radical Catholic counter-culturalism engaged in 'fifth-column', 'sabotage' activities and non-traditional formal choices in poetry: on the contrary, the latter serve the former.

However, Griffin does not consider the possibility of a Catholic Modernism: his approach to Christianity in general is typified by his remark that in the latter half of the nineteenth century 'the crisis of the credibility of both Christianity and the progress myth as stable sources of transcendence deepened' (Griffin 2007: 110) as a preliminary to modernity beginning to be experienced in terms of decadence. For Jones and his Catholic milieu, though, Catholicism was no mere relic of the past, but rather a potential force of rebirth and revolution no less than – *though distinct from* – fascism. Elizabeth Ward accuses Jones of being near-fascist, whereas Thomas Dilworth, quoting and contextualizing a nearly 20-page unpublished essay on Hitler written by Jones in May 1939, vigorously defends him from the charge. More interesting in this context is that the essay, and a related letter to Harman Grisewood a month before, serve to distinguish Jones and his milieu intellectually from Hitler, even as it is foolishly arguing for increased 'understanding and sympathy' (Jones, quoted in Dilworth 1986: 155) in Britain, at that anxious time, for the dictator's motives and the 'Fascist and Nazi revolutions':

> In reading *Mein Kampf* I was often reminded of the problems I used to hear discussed continuously by various groups of Catholic people concerning the recovery of social justice: how to break the 'chain store', how to live uncorrupted by the 'banking system', how to free men from the many and great evils of 'capitalist exploitation', how to effect some real and just relationship between the price of things and the labour expended. [...] All took it for granted that there existed powers inimical to a human way of life who were the enemy at any attempt at a solution, because of money interest and one thing and another. The whole system was said to be corrupt, unChristian, intolerable. [...] In the main, however, there was the idea that some sort of return to the Land was of great importance. [...] [The Fascist and Nazi revolutions] represent, for all their alarming characteristics, an heroic attempt to cope with certain admitted corruptions in our civilization. Even the terrible aspects of those regimes, the brutality and suppression of individual freedom, must at least be considered in relation to the nature and malignancy of the particular conditions and evils that those regimes set out to correct.
>
> (Jones, quoted in Dilworth 1986: 154–5)

Dilworth rightly points out that Jones is not advocating fascism, but appeasement;[46] that in the wartime fragments later published as 'The Wall' and the 'The Tutelar of the Place' he is distinctly hostile to *Gleichschaltung*, the Nazi term for forcible central coordination (150); and that he was horrified by Nazi war atrocities (159), admitting he had been wrong about Hitler. In the above-mentioned letter to Grisewood (4 October 1938), significantly a private communication rather than a public apologia for Hitler, Jones notes that 'this *hate* thing mars his whole thing [...] the world as just going on *for ever* in this steel grip', and that 'the conception of the world in terms of the race-struggle (that's what it boils down to) will hardly do' (quoted in Dilworth 1986: 158). Ultimately, then, 'Compared with his opponents he is grand, but compared with the saints he is bloody. And I think I mean also by saints – lovers, and all kinds of unifying makers. Anyway, I back him still against all this currish, leftish, money thing' (quoted in Dilworth 1986: 158). As Ward observes, Jones's thought is so permeated by the framework of civilizational crisis that he is 'blinded [...] to the true polarities of contemporary European politics' (Ward 1983: 62) and to the real differences between regimes.

Jones's political naïveté aside, his case is a clear example of 'Griffinite' Modernism that is nonetheless unexplored by Griffin: the 'problem' identified (modern decadence, search for renewal) is for Jones related in many respects to the fascist one, but the 'solution' must be different for the Catholic Modernist. On one level, Jones has no solution, at least not politically, and this is part of the reason for his desultory fascination with Hitler as man-of-action. On another, his solution is to affirm through his work – as it were behind enemy lines – the values of the artist, the saint, the lover, the unifying maker. A later text speaks of Jones's self-conception as a modern Boethius, 'who has been nicknamed "the Bridge", because he carried forward into an altogether metamorphosed world certain of the fading oracles which had sustained antiquity' (DJDG, 11); the bridge here leads to an unknown future in which the oracles' voices may again be heard.

Looking beyond Jones himself, one can see here the contours of an entire distinct field of study emerging. Even within Jones's immediate milieu, there were of course as many variations on the basic 'problem' of the 'admitted corruptions' of modern civilization, and as many possible solutions (artistic, intellectual or directly political), as there were individuals.[47] Simply to wave the labels 'proto-fascist' or 'nostalgia' at them fails to capture any nuances here. If we move beyond this group, and Catholicism itself, to the wider Christian scene, Chapter 3 of this book examines the revitalization of Christian dogma for contemporary use in T. S. Eliot and W. H. Auden. Furthermore, while Eliot was distinctly right-leaning (though, I will argue, *less* inclined towards fascism after his conversion than before), Auden's sympathies are with the liberal left and with democracy: for Auden, Western democracy needed acutely to regenerate itself by reconnecting with its Christian roots. So although many 'Griffinite Christian Modernists' were in fact right-leaning, there is no *necessary* link here: we will find Auden, too, decrying the 'failure of liberal capitalist democracy', since 'by denying the social nature of personality, and by ignoring the social power of money, it has created the most impersonal, the most mechanical and the most unequal civilization the world has ever seen' (APr II: 6–7). This whole category of 'Christian Modernists', then, demands much broader, more detailed and comparative study of a range of individuals and movements. The present book can only scratch the surface.

However, while Jones's case lends itself well to analysis in Griffin's terms with minor modifications, Joyce's Modernism poses an important challenge to such analysis. This is chiefly so because the idea that modernity is inherently threatening, rotten, sick or decadent is very hard to fit onto the work of this iconic Modernist. Let Leopold Bloom's amiable utopia, the New Bloomosalem, serve as an indicator here:

> Union of all, jew, moslem and gentile. Three acres and a cow for all children of nature. Saloon motor hearses. Compulsory manual labour for all. All parks open to the public day and night. Electric dishscrubbers. Tuberculosis, lunacy, war and mendicancy must now cease. General amnesty, weekly carnival with masked license, bonuses for all, esperanto the universal language with universal brotherhood. No more patriotism of barspongers and dropsical impostors. Free money, free rent, free love and a free lay church in a free lay state.
>
> (JJU, 462)

While parodic, Bloom's distinctly internationalist vision of an Esperanto-speaking universal brotherhood is also a serious rebuke to those insisting on distinctions of 'race' and religion, with additional swipes at patriotism, war and other lunacy, and restrictions on 'free love' and even 'masked license'. Advocacy of motored hearses, electric dish-scrubbers and the end of tuberculosis reveal a practical, unsentimental attitude to the benefits of modern machinery and medicine. The combination of 'free money, free rent' and 'compulsory manual labour' invokes the anarchist-communist motto 'from each according to his means, to each according to his needs' (Mangianello 1980: 111). Finally, a 'free lay church in a free lay state' implies freedom from compulsion from either church or state in all matters of faith, and a democratic vision of religious pluralism. These utopian features are all distinct products of Western modernity, and it is also worth noting the defiantly heroic status of Bloom in *Ulysses*: for the figure of the 'international' atheist Jew – that 'Capitalist-Bolshevist' phantasm – was widely reviled and abused as the fomenter of decadence in this period.[48] It seems, then, that Joyce's playful representation of utopia implies that many aspects of modernity should be embraced and accelerated; though clearly any Joycean (not just Bloomian) utopia would also include the continued freedom to treat the very notion of utopia playfully.

Griffin's theory thus seems at first sight too inflexible to fit Joyce's liberal, left-leaning, 'pro-modernity' Modernism.[49] Yet there *is* a distinctive crisis of decadence, or societal and mental 'paralysis', at work in Joyce's fictional universe. Joyce famously told his brother, 'What's the matter with you is that you're afraid to live. You and people like you. This city is suffering from hemiplegia of the will' (quoted in Walzl 1961: 221). Again, the title of the short-story collection *Dubliners* was intended to 'betray the soul of that hemiplegia or paralysis which many consider a city' (letter to Grant Richards, 5 May 1906, quoted in Walzl 1961: 221). Florence L. Walzl points out that implicit in Joyce's scheme of illustrating this paralysis under the four aspects of childhood, adolescence, maturity and public life was 'a personification of Ireland as a sick, even moribund individual'. Indeed, Joyce spoke of the 'special odour of corruption' surrounding his stories (222). As Walzl notes, throughout the collection, images of 'living death, or rather succession of deaths, emotional, psychological, or spiritual, details of darkness, cold, night, winter and blindness' are contrasted with 'the motif of life, which for Joyce meant vital action or escape [. . .] symbolized by images of growth, light, motion, water, or flight' (223). The binary opposition of darkness and death versus light and New Life at work here is just as apocalyptic as in an 'anti-modernity' Modernist such as Jones: *but with Joyce the root cause of cultural sickness is not modernity, but the Catholic Church, and New Life is to be sought by opposing it.* Emblematically, in 'The Sisters', the young boy who has been taught by an elderly priest ('a disappointed man' gone in his mind by the end) names the sickness on the very first page, for after the priest's death, 'Every night as I gazed up at the window I said softly to myself the word *paralysis*' (JJD, 1). Though the old man had 'a great wish' for him, that is, the priesthood, the boy is 'freed from something by his death' (4).

At this point, we should recall Finn Fordham's focus on how opposition to the ultramontanist Catholic Church became a rallying point for any number of cultural Modernists of various tendencies – explicit in the call for a final battle between the 'modern and medieval ways of thought' in *The New Age*. More generally, the negatively unifying role of Christianity as looming, powerful antagonist and as symbol of everything that is corrupt and moribund and still-to-be-overcome before some desired variant of a redeemed Western modernity ensues, has been given insufficient attention within Modernist studies. Accordingly, Roger Griffin's theory, useful as it is in identifying the pattern of 'futurally' oriented sickness-and-cure, or corruption-and-renewal thinking that so permeates Modernism – and the Modernism of the Right in particular – would still seem to need supplementation in two ways. First, as we have seen, it does not explicitly acknowledge that Christianity itself can function as 'revitalizing' agent for some Modernists. Griffin instead relegates its influence too simply to the past. Second, for many other Modernist groups, traditional Christianity, and *not* necessarily modernity per se, was considered the root cause and dominant symbol of cultural illness, which of course affected the direction of the many cures proposed as well. While all Modernists opposed the status quo, and invoked the idea of present cultural crisis, the aim of some was an intensified, triumphant modernity suitably cleansed of any remaining 'nostalgia' for the Christian past, or sympathy for 'reactionary' cultural politics in general.

Returning to Joyce and *Dubliners*, however, another complication appears. While Catholicism may be depicted as the root cause of this society's sickness, there is also an accretion of symbolism around this 'condition' that is not *necessarily* connected with the Church itself. In the final story, 'The Dead', religious matters are in the background, whereas the superficial hospitality of the party becomes the central symbol, as Walzl says, of 'a devitalized culture' wherein 'the people are intensely provincial, conformist, and materialistic in their enjoyments' (Walzl 1961: 228). Gabriel Conroy at the end is going down among the living dead, for having never (like his sleeping wife) been caught up in 'the full glory of some passion', he feels his identity 'fading out into a grey impalpable world' (JJD, 225). Yet in 'Eveline', the power of conventional mores is explicitly connected with the Church, as the heroine rejects escape with her lover by not boarding the boat to Buenos Aires whilst she prays 'to God to direct her, to show her what was her duty', ending up 'passive, like a helpless animal', devoid of love (34). In 'Grace', the concluding sermon conjures a debased, materialistic Christianity that has replaced all pretence at evangelism with accountancy: 'If he might use the metaphor, [the priest] said, he was their spiritual accountant; and he wished each and every one of his hearers to open his books, the books of his spiritual life, and see if they tallied accurately with conscience' (174). This seems to be a religion that aims only to keep the men in the pew 'on the books' a while longer, although its time is really past.

A useful tool for coming to grips with the subtle association between Church and cultural condition here is Toril Moi's emphasis on revolt against the surprisingly dominant late nineteenth-century ethical-aesthetic code of 'idealism' as a determining factor in the development of cultural Modernism. Moi argues that 'for half a century after the death of romanticism proper, an increasingly impoverished, moralizing, didactic form of idealism continued to function as a more or less compulsory master discourse about literature and art' (Moi 2006: 82). Romantics like Schiller had sought to reconcile the Kantian binaries of freedom and necessity through art, in order to 'uplift and ennoble us, to give us concrete visions of a better world with better human beings in it' (75). However, Moi pinpoints the 'faultlines' in this view:

> The representation of human sexuality *requires* idealization, or it will be vulgar. In order to become properly poetic, sex must be sublimated, ennobled, and beautified, that is to say it must be turned into highly idealized love. [...] In order to avoid the coarse and the vulgar, consciousness must transcend the body; morality, duty, and will must conquer mere material nature. (79)

Hence the figure of the 'pure woman', ready to 'sacrifice her life for love' (79). The Joycean connection here is obvious when recalling his invective, quoted earlier, against the 'lying drivel about pure men and pure women and spiritual love and love for ever',[50] and his admiration for Ibsen's realism is not hard to understand. A key driver of Modernism on Moi's reading is 'the idea that idealism might be destructive and demoralizing, rather than uplifting and harmonizing' (Moi 2006: 85). Thus naturalists saw the search for 'truth' and 'reality' precisely as 'antidotes to idealism'. The Art-for-art's-sake movement provocatively severed the link between beauty and moral ideals, whereas 'Baudelaire's attempt to produce beauty out of evil and Flaubert's nihilistic irony both attacked the very core of idealist aesthetics, and both produced a new and unsettling understanding of the purpose of art, pointing in the direction of a modern anti-idealist formalism' (90). The establishment reaction, for instance in anti-naturalist polemics, 'conveys an overwhelming sense that beauty has been blemished, innocence defiled, womanhood dishonored, God defied', via 'an unusually insistent and widespread imagery of dirt, manure, sickness, boils, sores, infection, rotting corpses, and sexual depravation' (90).

Part of what is happening in *Dubliners* is that the imagery of corruption and death is being turned back on the 'idealizers', and more generally on Dublin considered as a bourgeois, parochial, materialistic society that is in the grip of a purely conventional, oppressive moralist-aesthetic discourse. Against this background, it is easy to see that Joyce's lifelong preoccupation with developing an alternative literary language – his intensifying assault on 'wideawake language, cutanddry grammar and goahead plot'[51] that would culminate in *Finnegans Wake* – is no 'mere' formal exercise, but has clear cultural and political implications.[52] Furthermore, Joyce's overall diagnosis, making the Church the root cause of Dublin's cultural illness, is a highly polemical one. Moi notes that 'because nineteenth-century idealists almost always fused morality and religion, anti-idealists were almost always taken to be freethinkers or worse' (Moi 2006: 71), but it is a weakness in her account that she never questions whether such a fusion of the languages of 'idealism' and religion might itself be challenged by contemporaries inclined towards a more radical, counter-cultural and revitalized Christianity. By contrast, there is an implicit sense in Joyce's story 'Grace' that religion has indeed become debased here, and we know that he had considerable respect for the past theological giants of the Church like Thomas Aquinas, finding them 'suggestive of thought even when he did not agree with them' (Stanislaus Joyce, quoted in Lernout 2010: 101). But he was also content, in this cultural war, to make use of the freethinker's weaponry, which included blaming the Church for the ascendancy of the idealist-religious complex that he despised. However, Moi's whole perspective here is useful precisely in alerting the critic to the fact that for those Modernists who rallied against Christianity as a common enemy to be overcome in the name of a purified and intensified Western modernity, the Church is not the *sole* target: rather, the whole idealist-religious complex is usually at stake.

For an example of a Modernist who resists 'idealist' language even while embracing Christianity, we turn again to David Jones. As noted before, the aesthetic philosophy of Maritain enabled a whole post-war generation of Catholic artists in France to develop a 'dialectical realism' that could incorporate the grotesque, the ugly and the dissonant into art without sentimentalization. Even in a shattered humanity or a culture in ruins, traces necessarily remain of our more original nature as *artifex*. Now, as an ex-serviceman in the Great War, Jones was acutely aware of how 'high-falutin', bombastic, speciously idealistic language' was exploited in propaganda slogans such as 'Honour is above peace' (quoted in Dilworth 1986: 156) to encourage self-sacrifice, even while the merciless technologies of machine guns and poison gas dehumanized the troops on both sides and made a mockery of that sacrifice. His war poem *In Parenthesis* tries to 'see formal goodness in a life singularly inimical, hateful to us' (DJIP, xiii) by salvaging 'sacramental' signs from the cultural history and wartime realities of 'man-the-maker'. But Jones's 'formal goodness' in no way resembles the programmatic, pre-defined 'uplift', 'enno-blement', 'harmony' and exhortations to 'duty' and 'self-sacrifice' that Moi identifies in late nineteenth-century idealism. The goodness in question is rather ontological. In part III, there is an unsettling anal-ogy between the 'rat of no-man's land' and the soldiers: 'These too have shed their fine feathers; these too have slimed their dark-bright coats; these too have condescended to dig in' (DJIP, 54). The rats can be heard feasting on corpses, 'by a rule of his nature / at night-feast on the broken of us'; yet they 'suffer with us this metamorphosis' (54). That is, the natures of both rats and humans are still indelible gifts of the Creator, and the human gift of symbolic metamorphosis – turn-ing rat-life into a metaphor of soldiering – cannot be extinguished even at this extreme.

For Jones, both art and religion are necessarily engaged in 'fifth-column', 'sabotage' activity within the hostile environment of modern civilization: they are 'disruptive forces', 'irritants', a sign of 'contradiction'. On the side of religion, Christ's words in Matthew's Gospel spring to mind: 'You are the salt of the earth. But if the salt lose its savour, wherewith shall it be salted? It is good for nothing any more but to be cast out and to be trodden on by men' (Matt. 5:13).[53] The association between the Church and any conventionalized, culturally specific discourse such as Moi's moral-aesthetic 'idealism' is bound to remain unstable, since the Gospels themselves contain a radical counter-cultural message that can always be accessed anew. This will-ingness to be the 'salt of the earth' rather than conform to the modern status quo distinguishes Jones from more establishment-figure, con-ventional Christians of his day. With regard to art, it is important to note that Jones approved of a range of distinctly anti-'idealistic', experimental Modernist forms as part and parcel of this project of cultural 'disruption', even where their ideology did not match his own; but he did not have any interest in the kind of anti-naturalist polemics cited by Moi. In 1952 he drafted a letter to *The Listener* which includes an interesting list of favourites in response to a previous, quite philistine letter attacking non-representational art per se:

The astringency and punch of Pound and Wyndham Lewis from 1914 and onwards, the moving serenities of Ben Nicholson's abstractions of to-day, the terse forms of the harbinger, GM Hopkins of 1880, the various feats of Picasso, the spell-binding and terminal achievement of Joyce . . . You may detest it all, but you cannot explain it away.[54]

This returns us to Joyce, and we will touch on Jones's idiosyncratic reading of that 'spell-binding' achievement in our concluding section. Our immediate task, however, is to test the critical utility of the idea of 'Catholic Modernism' further by comparing Joyce's *Ulysses* and Jones's *In Parenthesis* in terms of the interlocking themes of Eucharist and artistic creativity. These are central to both writers; but, given the sharp ideological contrasts between them charted here, what can really be learned from juxtaposing their work?

Eucharist and Art in *Ulysses* and *In Parenthesis*

The Church is made by me and my like – her services, legends, practices, paintings, music, traditions. These her artists gave her. They made her what she is.
                                        – James Joyce, *Stephen Hero* (JJSH, 143)

But properly speaking and at the root of the matter, Ars knows only a 'sacred' activity.
                                        – David Jones, 'Art and Sacrament' (DJEA, 157)

Neither *Ulysses* nor *In Parenthesis* is reducible to an ideological framework, for these works also interrogate those frameworks even to the brink of collapse, generating dramatic tension from the process. As Frederick K. Lang has argued in impressive detail,

Ulysses contains a simulacrum of the Mass. As a result the Mass itself is gradually transmuted into a rite of 'de-Consecration'. Mystical body and blood are supplanted by physical body and blood [. . .] Human flesh is the Eucharist of the Bloomsday Mass, and human rites, both biological and liturgical, constitute its liturgy.

                                        (Lang 1993: 106)

This strategy serves 'to aggrandize the human body, to declare human flesh sacramental' (138). Lang takes it for granted that Joyce is successful in that aim, but this tends to elide the staggering scale of Joyce's artistic ambition, and the considerable risk it involves. The quotation from *Stephen Hero* above indicates that the artist for Joyce is the

Maker of religion: *Ulysses* involves an attempt to unmake Catholicism via its own native imagery, thereby declaring itself as scripture, proclaiming the exaltation of fleshly, embodied human creativity for a dawning liberal modern era. But can a vast, age-old, influential 'artwork' such as the Catholic rites and traditions really be undone by one man's modern epic? Will the impressiveness and conviction of the case for the 'sacramentalization' of the flesh remain in some sense parasitic on the Catholic imagery employed to convey it, however subversively that imagery is treated? And does the very creativity asserted in constructing this vision thereby retain some indelible aura of the sacred that does not sit so easily with a materialist philosophy? The last question evokes Jones's claim from 'Art and Sacrament' that 'Ars' finally knows only a 'sacred' activity; and Jones's aesthetic starting point seems inversely to mirror Joyce's residual anxiety here. Yet Jones's prose poem contains its own anxieties about the validity of that premise as it is confronted with the Great War. Thomas Dilworth's helpful reading demonstrates the epic ambition of the liturgical analogy at work here:

> *In Parenthesis* opens in the weeks before Christmas and closes in the summer's battle. On this opening and closing, liturgical analogues impose patterns of inception and completion, promise and fulfilment. [...] Evocations of the Nativity at Christmas are answered during the battle by allusions to Good Friday. Advent anticipates apocalypse in the first half of the poem: battle metaphorically fulfils that anticipation.
>
> (Dilworth 1979: 4)

Dilworth quotes a letter from Jones to René Hague saying that 'all our miseries and sufferings can be seen as in some way part of the whole anabasis and passion' of Christ (in Dilworth 1979: 22), but in the poem itself, the analogy is not merely assumed but rigorously tested. How can Christ's 'going-up' towards the cross ('anabasis' recalls a military march) and his passion – re-presented in the sacrifice of the Mass – still be relevant *here*? Does it perhaps resolve itself into another defunct artistic mythology – or can Christ truly be discovered 'in the order of signs'? Neither *Ulysses* nor *In Parenthesis* offers any stable position that can simply dispel the ambiguities which haunt them, however much we as critics would prefer to have our own preconceptions confirmed by these texts. Instead, comparison offers a wider perspective by which the tensions within each work stand out in clearer relief when viewed through the mirror of the other. Such a perspective helps us discern precisely how the intimate confrontation with the vast and intricate system of Catholic faith and ritual shapes the creative work of both these 'Catholic Modernist' writers.

Space permits only the briefest thematic sketch of *Ulysses* here, drawing on Lang's lovingly detailed study, and geared towards comparisons between Joyce and Jones. One underlying scheme of great importance to the novel is the instigation of a transformation of the Joycean alter ego Stephen Dedalus into the future 'creator of *Ulysses*' through the ministrations of Leopold Bloom and implicitly also Bloom's wife Molly. At the start of the novel, Stephen is stuck: although a self-confessed 'horrible example of free thought' (JJU, 20), he constantly broods over theological categories and obscure points of Church ritual and history, while suffering obsessive guilt over his failure to give in to propriety and kneel to pray at his mother's deathbed. He thinks of escape from his three masters, Ireland, the British Empire and the Roman Catholic Church, but for the moment fritters away his time with the likes of Buck Mulligan, spendthrift and provocative Nietzschean mocker of religion. A chain of images unfolding across the first three chapters sums up his situation. On the opening page, Mulligan turns his morning shave into a mock-mass, presenting his mirror as paten for the Eucharistic 'host' (his razor): he calls Stephen 'poor dogsbody' (JJU, 6), an anagram of 'God's body', and as Stephen looks in the same mirror (himself figuring as the host) he repeats the phrase. In the 'Proteus' chapter, the image returns to become a focus of Stephen's meditations upon a dog carcass on the beach ('poor dogsbody's body' (46)), metamorphosing into a vision of world-flesh and God-flesh finally identical and equally rotten: 'God becomes man becomes fish becomes barnacle goose becomes featherbed mountain. Dead breaths I living breathe, tread dead dust, devour a ruinous offal from all dead' (49). Despite his 'freethinking', Stephen is far from the fleshly YES pronounced by Molly Bloom at the end of the novel: his residual Catholicism riddles him with self-disgust, guilt and revulsion towards the world. But becoming a mere mocker like Mulligan would not solve this problem: he must instead go *through* Catholic symbols and appropriate their power in order imaginatively to redeem the flesh – and *Ulysses* itself is the outcome of that process.

As in *Dubliners*, then, Catholicism is associated with death and repression, and the New Life must be won by overcoming it. In *Ulysses*, the invention of the atheist Jew Leopold Bloom, an outsider to the Church who is able to observe its rituals and dogmas with-out the intense personal involvement of Stephen, accordingly pro-vides a vantage point 'beyond' Catholicism. However, Bloom is also repeatedly associated with aspects of the Catholic liturgy. In the fifth chapter, 'Lotos-eaters', Bloom attends Mass, observing the drug-like effects of the rituals on the believers: 'The priest bent down to put it into her mouth, murmuring all the time. Latin. [...] What? *Corpus*. Body. Corpse. Good idea the Latin. Stupefies them first. [...] Rum idea: eating bits of a corpse why the cannibals cotton to it' (JJU, 77). As critics have noted, there is something of the anthropological observer about Bloom here, though his observa-tions also have a sharp sting of critique. Continuing the theme of 'stupefaction', he muses on the group psychology of communion ('like one family party', 'not so lonely', 'blind faith', 'lulls all pain' (JJU, 78)), and on confession as mind-control ('Punish me please. Great weapon in their hands' (79)), while registering a certain hor-ror at the implicit 'cannibalism' and the celebration of a human sacrifice in the Mass (mistranslating I.N.R.I. as 'Iron nails ran in' (78)). Bloom's counter-reaction is to fantasize about masturbating in the bath: the 'stream of life' is associated with the 'gentle tepid stream' of water, and with the spent gush of semen surrounding his 'limp father of thousands': 'This is my body' (83). The critique of a deathly Catholicism continues as Bloom attends the funeral of Paddy Dignam: the rituals revolve around the next world, paradise and resurrection, but for Bloom this is unconvincing. As he sees it, the focus on death and the afterlife merely distracts from embodied life here and now:

> Give you the creeps after a bit. I will appear to you after death [...] There is another world after death named hell. I do not like that other world [Martha] wrote. No more do I. Plenty to see and hear and feel yet. Feel live warm beings near you. Let them sleep in their maggoty beds. They are not going to get me this innings. Warm beds: warm fullblooded life. (110)

As Lang shows, the Eucharistic intimations surrounding Bloom are fulfilled in the 'Nausicaa' episode, when Bloom does masturbate, to the sight of young Gerty MacDowell at the beach raising her skirt for his viewing pleasure, even as the Blessed Sacrament is being ele-vated in the nearby church of Our Lady Star of the Sea during the Benediction service: 'Consecration becomes masturbation and Eleva-tion becomes erection' (Lang 1993: 172). Accordingly, 'Bloom's body replaces the body of Christ, and like Christ, Bloom is celebrant as well as sacramental body [...] The transubstantiation of the wine is also paralleled in "Nausicaa". This is the first day of Gerty's period, her monthly shedding of blood' (173). This second 'consecration' will later find a parallel in Molly Bloom's menstruation, as she 'becomes fleshly Eucharist by fulfilling upon her chamberpot the prophecy of mingling blood and water' (170; cf. John 19:34).

Bloom eventually assumes the role of father to Stephen, guiding him through a phantasmagoric 'harrowing of hell' among the prostitutes of 'Nighttown' and towards a 'resurrection' dawn and a 'communion' breakfast in 7 Eccles Street, a 'homely rather than holy communion' (Lang 1993: 258).[55] Molly stays upstairs but becomes part of their meal through her breakfast cream (symbolizing 'the cream of her breasts' (Lang 1993: 261)), mingled with Epp's cocoa (a 'massproduct' (JJU, 629)) and water: 'Molly's breakfast cream corresponds to the particle from the consecrated host that is mingled with and sanctifies the wine on Good Friday' (Lang 1993: 261). In the 'Penelope' chapter, Molly's final monologue gushes forth like the stream of life itself. Her triumphant fleshliness and sexuality counterpoints the aura of death and decomposition that has haunted the novel, but she also epitomizes verbal creativity. After his meeting with Stephen, Bloom will be able to return to marital communion with her after ten years of anxious abstinence following the death of his son Rudy; and Stephen, 'fathered' by Bloom and partaking mystically of Molly (whose real name, Marion, also links her to the Virgin Mary and the Incarnation), will be able to assume his role as Creator of the new Holy Scripture of *Ulysses* itself. However, the ambiguity of this ambition should by now be clear. If the ordinary can be named as the sacred only with the help of Catholic imagery, has the Old Testament (Catholicism) really given way to the New (liberalism, materialism)? Or, from another angle, how can the act of naming – the creative manipulation of signs – be fully shorn of any relation towards a transcendent Other, when that creative act is itself so persistently associated with figurations of the Creator? Of course, readers must finally answer such questions for themselves, but they do return us to the book's starting point: how to assess Stephen Dedalus's ferocious *agon* with the Catholic religion.

In Parenthesis revolves around a constant search for traces of the sacred within ordinary sign-making, and, through this, for the Christ who entered 'into the order of signs'. The poem's method here distinguishes itself sharply from the official religion presented to the soldiers on a Sunday:

> The official service was held in the field; there they had spreaded a Union Jack on piled biscuit tins, behind the 8 in. siege, whose regular discharges made quite inaudible the careful artistry of the prayers he read.
>
> He preached from the Matthew text, of how He cares for us above the sparrows. The medical officer undid, and did up again, the fastener of his left glove, behind his back, throughout the whole discourse. They sang *Onward Christian Soldiers* for the closing hymn.

(DJIP, 107)

The Union Jack has replaced the altar cloth, and the makeshift altar itself is a pile of factory-produced tins piled behind a discharging siege gun; the machine destroys the only remaining 'artistry' within this service. Religion is subservient to utility and propaganda: the medical officer, who has seen the worst of the war, fidgets at the useless cold comfort of the sermon, and Baring-Gould's eschatological hymn about the Church Militant is glibly identified with the present war effort. The many parallels between the life of soldiers and the Catholic liturgy in Jones's poem will strive to avoid this kind of propaganda. Instead, starting from unconscious, spontaneous, observable patterns within one regiment's life, the liturgical analogies register both similarities and disturbing disjunctions. Can this religious language still speak about the realities of modern war? And can Christ's salvific action be discerned even in the grisly panorama of such a war?

In general, as Thomas Dilworth has shown, the daily rituals of soldiering are described in terms evoking Eucharistic fellowship and communion. The most explicit example is the distribution of supplies on Christmas morning:

> Come off it Moses – dole out the issue.
> Dispense salvation,
> Strictly apportion it,
> let us taste and see,
> let us be renewed,
> for Christ's sake let us be warm.

(DJIP, 73)

As Dilworth notes, the name Moses here 'recalls the prefiguration of the Eucharist in the saving quail and "bread from heaven" that were rationed to the starving Israelites (Exodus 16)' (Dilworth 1979: 5). Echoing this moment before the onset of battle, 'a meal consisting of unleavened seed-cake is shared by [Private] Ball and his friends. "In haste they ate it" [DJIP, 146], as the Passover meal was eaten before the coming of the angel of death' (Dilworth 1979: 6). In part I, we hear of 'the silence peculiar to parade grounds and refectories' (DJIP, 1), and like an abbot's authority, 'a lance-corporal's stripe is but held vicariously and from on high, is of one texture with an eternal economy' (2). As orders are shouted and the marching begins, there is 'the concerted movement of arms in which the spoken word effected what it signified' (3), like the sacramental words of a priest. Thus, 'The liturgy of a regiment departing has been sung' (4). In part III, this training will be put into practice, and despite the dangers ahead, this entails 'a kind of blessedness [. . .] a whole unlovely order this night would transubstantiate, lend some grace to' (27). They have learned their trade as soldiers, and thus 'the newness, the pressure of sudden, modifying circumstance [. . .] brought intelligibility and effectiveness to the used formulae of command; the liturgy of their going-up assumed a primitive creativeness, an apostolic actuality, a correspondence with the object, a flexibility' (28). The focus in such imagery is on 'man the maker' and his arts of war, with deep roots in the past. But this whole creative order is in danger of obliteration in this new war: as Jones put it in the Preface, 'We feel a rubicon has been passed between striking with a hand weapon as men used to do and loosing poison from the sky as we do ourselves' (DJIP, xiv).

The words about authority held from on high in part I also contain an unsettling echo of Christ's reply to Pilate's assertion that he has the power to crucify him: 'Thou shouldst not have any power against me, unless it were given thee from above' (John 19:11). Part III opens by citing the rubrics from the Good Friday liturgy ('No blessing is asked, neither is the kiss of peace given' (DJIP, 27)). The implication is that the crucifixion experience of this battle too would not happen unless allowed from above, and that the 'going-up', the anabasis, is somehow a necessary rite. Yet how does the grotesque dehumanization of this war still connect with Christ's sacrifice? Bodies are everywhere mangled and destroyed without burial, 'precious, patient of baptism; chemical-corrupted once-bodies', 'dung-making Holy Ghost temples' (43). As Dilworth points out, this contravenes 'the principal sign of hope in resurrection, the burial of the dead' (Dilworth 1979: 12). The unknown soldier – 'Johnny' – is likened to Christ via Isaiah 53:2 ('there is no beauty in him, nor comeliness [. . .]

there was no sightliness, that we should be desirous of him'), yet the faceless anonymity of this destruction seems to question the possibility of any resurrected identity: 'They've served him barbarously – poor Johnny – you wouldn't desire him, you wouldn't know him for any other' (DJIP, 43).

Dilworth draws attention to the connected imagery of Advent in the first three parts of the poem, and apocalypse in the final sections: 'Advent, of course, anticipates the feast of the Incarnation, but it derives much of its character from the apocalyptic vision of the last Sunday of Pentecost, and its major concern is with the coming of Christ and the Last Judgment' (Dilworth 1979: 14). However, he does not fully bring out the irony of this conjunction, for this is an Advent without any Nativity,[56] and the 'prearranged hour of apocalypse' (DJIP, 135) is a mechanical simulacrum followed by no general resurrection:

> Riders on pale horses loosed
> and vials irreparably broken
> an' Wat price bleedin' Glory
> Glory
> Glory Hallelujah
>
> (DJIP, 160)

Of course, Dilworth here identifies the horsemen of Revelation 6:8, and the 'seven golden vials full of the wrath of God' from Revelation 16. But if the vials are *irreparably broken* in this earthly battle, then the real Judgement may not be forthcoming, and 'Glory' is just a bleedin' song. This anxiety must be admitted into the poem, for only then can we appreciate that its images do not simply assert that the Christian pattern fits these events, but are the instruments of an ongoing, pressing search for Christ 'at the turn of a civilization'. Waiting for the one who is to return 'to judge the quick and the dead' can be like a desperate fumble in a dark wood under fire:

> No longer light of day on the quick and the dead but blindfold beating the air and tentative step by step deployment of the shades; grope in extended line of platoon through nether glooms concentrically, trapes phantom flares, warily circumambulate malignant miraged obstacles, walk confidently into hard junk. Solid things dissolve, and vapours ape substantiality.
>
> (DJIP, 179)

In both *Ulysses* and *In Parenthesis*, sacramental associations are used to affirm the value of ordinary, embodied human life. Furthermore, in both works creativity and sign-making stand opposed to deathliness and annihilation. At the same time, both works contain unresolved tensions about the validity and success of the creative methods they employ to present these values. The question remains for each author: can the Catholic imagery bear the specific weight and emphasis they place upon it? Reading these texts alongside each other is thus to realize the complexity and fascination of 'Catholic Modernism' as a distinct object of study.

Conclusion:
Influence, Affinity and Catholic Modernisms

Despite the thematic affinities between *Ulysses* and *In Parenthesis*, Joyce's famous novel did not influence Jones's composition of his prose poem, for the simple reason that he had not read *Ulysses* at the time. There was, however, a quite distinct Joycean influence upon Jones, through his encounter (around 1928) with the 'Anna Livia Plurabelle' episode from what was then known as *Work in Progress*, and later his close study of the whole of *Finnegans Wake* from the late 1930s through to the 1950s, eventually with the aid of studies like Joseph Campbell and Henry M. Robinson's *A Skeleton Key to Finnegans Wake* (1944). Jones was particularly fascinated with Joyce's recording of this episode, which he listened to over and over, and claimed at one point (in 1939) to have learned by heart. Of course, this direct influence (not least upon the 1952 poem *The Anathemata*) has been thoroughly scrutinized by Jones scholars.[57] Our purpose here is merely to indicate the idiosyncratic nature of Jones's reading of Joyce as a starting point for some general concluding reflections on methodological approaches to the phenomenon of 'Catholic Modernisms'.

While the opposing cultural stances of Jones and Joyce have been thoroughly documented above, Jones himself assimilated Joyce to his own interests: in a retrospective piece called 'Notes on the 1930s', he argued that while Joyce may have seemed 'so "cosmopolitan" a figure and highly "contemporary" and *thought of* by many as "a rebel" destructive of standards of all sorts, and enemy of tradition, etc.' (DJDG, 46), the reality was quite different. According to Jones, while Joyce drew on anthropological and archaeological study, on the new psychology of Freud and Jung, and on medieval scholasticism, the most important thing about his art is its rootedness in Dublin and, as we shall see, by implication the Celtic world. Joyce is an artist who,

> more than any other, for all the universality of his theme, depended upon a given locality [...] and the complex historic strata special to that site, to express a universal concept. It was from the *particular* that he made the *general* shine out. That is to say he was quintessentially 'incarnational'. (46)

Jones gives the example of how the Dublin street name Suffolk Place, conjoined with the Norse word for assembly, *Thing*, produces a striking sentence in 'Anna Livia Plurabelle': 'Northmen's thing make southfolk's place' (quoted in DJDG, 48). This epitomizes a continuing 'liaison with a whole complex of layers and strata of centuries', and thus Joyce's work conveyed a sense 'that liaison with the whole past of man-the-artist was still possible however "contemporary" the images employed' (48) – bringing us right back to Jones's own aesthetic programme. A longer, unpublished statement elaborates Jones's reading of Joyce (underline in original):

> The <u>as</u>tonishing thing (to me) about Joyce is that somehow or other, in the 20th Century, in an art so totally other, not as to medium, but in intention, and essentially cosmopolitan and influenced by that 19th Cent. Scandinavian play-wright (whose name I can never remember, though it's on the tip of my tongue) should have displayed to a unique degree this obsession for hard, exact, complex, intermeddled, cyclic form–content content–form. [...] In <u>his</u> case, at all events, the 'haecceity' of Scotus, and the syllogistic Thomist–Aristotelian framework (however procrustean the bed) did conjoin with the equally exacting, however differing, immemorial <u>disciplinae</u> of authentic Celtdom. We may not 'like' the result as it fully emerges in <u>Finnegans</u> Wake. [...] But that is hardly the point. The Thing exists, that is the way he made it, presumably the only way he could make it. And what emerges is an artwork of incredible complexity, universal in its content (in as far as one can, with great labour, discern some of these multiplicity of 'meanings') but more totally bound and conditioned by a given site & place & people than any other work one knows of, and its mode of construction turns out to be cyclic, turning in and round & about and 'ending' where it 'began' or rather having strictly speaking neither end nor beginning but interlacing like those knot-patterns so favoured of the Celts. And of course there is direct evidence of the 'influence' (I'm so bored with that word!) of the <u>Tunc</u> page in the Kell's Gospel-book.[58]

The 'disciplinae of authentic Celtdom' matter intensely to Jones because of his own deployment of Welsh myth and history, and because Joyce's complex 'cyclic form–content content–form' in *Finnegans Wake* offered him a model of modern experimental writing rooted in a specific place and connected with the 'immemorial' past of man-the-maker. In this light, Joyce's 'cosmopolitanism' and his relations with some nineteenth-century Scandinavian playwright can be waved aside.

The scholar must, of course, be less cavalier about 'influence' than the artist. This chapter has identified documentation of the precise role of all things Catholic in the biography, thought and aesthetic practice of individual artists as basic to the study of 'Catholic Modernisms'; and the same principle obviously applies to lines of influence between artists like Joyce and Jones themselves. As seen in the Jones extract just quoted, archival study offers a powerful tool here, combined with dense contextualization more generally. Yet Jones's attitude is instructive, since it shows so clearly how ideological differences between cultural Modernists may be downplayed by being assimilated to a different, idiosyncratic set of problems: thus an atheist can very well 'influence' a Christian, and vice versa. One characteristic of the 'Catholic Modernist', and the Christian Modernist more generally as opposed to more culturally conservative Christians, is precisely the willingness to assimilate a range of experimental, provocative work in this fashion. Once the lines of influence have been thoroughly established, however, it becomes all the more interesting to examine cases of affinity. As with the juxtaposition of *Ulysses* and *In Parenthesis*, such cases can function as effective thematic mirrors and contribute to a broader taxonomy of Catholic Modernisms. Finally, 'Catholic Modernism' is a paradoxical construction that invites further theoretical work. One aspect of the paradox is that anti-Catholicism is itself part of the history and critical construction of cultural Modernism; but likewise important are the positive attractions of the Catholic system of beliefs and rituals, with its centrality to the whole history of Western culture. However, it also seems a fruitful paradox, in that our theoretical frameworks for understanding cultural Modernism at large – such as those of Griffin and Moi examined here – can be tested and refined by being confronted with the concept of Catholic Modernism, and of course with other cases beyond those of Joyce and Jones.

3

OLD DOGMAS FOR A NEW CRISIS? HELL, USURY AND INCARNATION IN T. S. ELIOT, EZRA POUND AND W. H. AUDEN

In 1939, on the cusp of war, W. H. Auden could, in Michael North's words, 'summarize in one paragraph what had become a familiar indictment' (North 1991: 2):

> The most obvious social fact of the last forty years is the failure of liberal capitalist democracy, based on the premises that every individual is born free and equal, each an absolute entity independent of all others; and that a formal political equality, the right to vote, the right to a fair trial, the right of free speech, is enough to guarantee his freedom of action in his relation with his fellow men. The results are only too familiar to us all. By denying the social nature of personality, and by ignoring the social power of money, it has created the most impersonal, the most mechanical and the most unequal civilisation the world has ever seen, a civilisation in which the only emotion common to all classes is a feeling of individual isolation from everyone else, a civilisation torn apart by the opposing emotions born of economic injustice, the just envy of the poor and the selfish terror of the rich.
>
> (APr II, 6–7)

The social and political crises of the 1930s – from the Economic Crisis and widespread unemployment to the rise of totalitarian regimes in

Russia, Italy and Germany, war in Spain, and a ruptured international order leading to global war – were felt by intellectuals like Auden to place a whole civilization on trial. The verdict remained uncertain. Would 'liberal capitalist democracy' survive, and did it even have a right to exist? Would one of the new political religions, socialism or fascism, sweep all before it in revolution or total war, to create a new order, and perhaps a New Man altogether?

The term 'political religion'[59] is used here to point to the fact that for many interwar intellectuals, an exclusively political analysis of this situation would have seemed insufficient: the crisis also came to be seen as a religious one, raising with great urgency the question of the survival of Europe's Christian heritage, as against a possible post-Christian future. Christianity could now plausibly be understood as providing an independent critique and historical analysis of *all* political 'isms'; as a bulwark against impending chaos; and as a vital source of values – offering its own regeneration cure[60] for the ills of social atomism and injustice, a technocratic, de-spiritualized civilization, and an impersonal and malfunctioning industrial capitalism. For those drawn to it, Christianity might now be opposed to *ersatz* secular religions of all kinds; but even for the more sceptical, it could seem a specially useful prop or provider of prestige and social cohesion for one or another of the ambitious political schemes circulating everywhere.

This chapter examines the role of certain Christian dogmas in the political thought, cultural theory and aesthetics of three leading Modernist poets during the 1930s and early 1940s: Hell, or final damnation, in T. S. Eliot, the medieval condemnation of usury for Ezra Pound and the Incarnation in W. H. Auden's work. Two of them were Christian converts, Eliot from Unitarianism and philosophical scepticism to Anglo-Catholicism in 1927, and Auden, as late as 1939–40, from a half-hearted socialism to a version of the Anglicanism of his upbringing, liturgically Anglo-Catholic, but theologically a coat of many colours. On the other hand, Pound elaborated his own idiosyncratic neo-pagan creed, but began to interest himself in the Roman Catholic Church over the 1930s, to the point where, in an unpublished article from 1940 he could claim (less than convincingly) not to deny 'any Catholic dogma' (Pound 1996b: 141). The very idea and function of 'dogma' is thus very different for each of these poets, and the particular doctrines under discussion here also engage a striking range of contexts within their work and thought. This creative investment means that it would be extremely simplistic to understand this interest in dogma as mere 'reversion' to pre-defined traditional formulae; for what is at stake is precisely the re-invention and re-application of old dogmas to a new crisis.

T. S. Eliot: The 'Daily Terror of Eternity'

In an essay from 1930, T. S. Eliot's paradoxical reading of that apostle of decadence, Charles Baudelaire, as engaged in 'discovering Christianity for himself' with something like 'theological innocence' (ElSE, 422) focuses on the use of blasphemy and the threat of damnation as germs of discovery in Baudelaire's work.[61] Eliot argues that 'Genuine blasphemy, genuine in spirit and not purely verbal, is the product of partial belief, and is as impossible to the complete atheist as to the perfect Christian. It is a way of affirming belief' (421). Baudelaire is thus concerned

> not with demons, black masses, and romantic blasphemy, but with the real problem of good and evil. [...] In the middle of the nineteenth century, the age which (at its best) Goethe had prefigured, an age of bustle, programmes, platforms, scientific progress, humanitarianism and revolutions which improved nothing, an age of progressive degradation, Baudelaire perceived that what really matters is Sin and Redemption. [... In fact,] the recognition of the reality of Sin is a New Life; and the possibility of damnation is so immense a relief in a world of electoral reform, plebiscites, sex reform and dress reform, that *damnation itself is an immediate form of salvation* – of salvation from the ennui of modern life, because it at last gives some significance to living. [... In] so far as we do evil or good, we are human; and it is better, in a paradoxical way, to do evil than to do nothing: at least, we exist. It is true to say that the glory of man is his capacity for salvation; *it is also true that his glory is his capacity for damnation.*
>
> (427, 429, my italics)

Eliot's vigorous attachment to the dogma of the human capacity for final damnation by God's supernatural authority in a real afterlife became a driving force for him, both on an intellectual and a deeply personal level. In a letter to his friend Paul Elmer More (2 June 1930) in response to More's comments on Eliot's 1929 Dante essay, we find the following:

> But, equally seriously, I am perturbed by your comments on Hell. To me it *is giustizia, sapienza, amore.* And I cannot help saying [...] that I am really

shocked by your assertion that God did not make Hell. It seems to me that you have lapsed into Humanitarianism. [...] To me, religion has brought at least the perception of something above morals, and therefore extremely terrifying; it has brought me not happiness, but the sense of something above happiness and therefore more terrifying than ordinary pain and misery; the very dark night and the desert. To me, the phrase 'to be damned for the glory of God' is sense not paradox; I had far rather walk, as I do, in daily terror of eternity, than feel that this was only a children's game in which all the contestants would get equally worthless prizes in the end. And I don't know whether this is to be labelled 'Classicism' or 'Romanticism': I only think that I have got hold of the tip of the tail of something quite real, more real than morals or than sweetness and light and culture.

(quoted in Jain 2004: 227–8)

What we have here is finally something quite extreme: *ennui* is more violently feared than Hell itself; in fact, it is simply unbearable.[62] But the perception is not merely a negative one, a flight: for Eliot, dogma also gives access, through faith, to 'something above morals', the *mysterium tremendum et fascinans*, the 'dark night and the desert' of a St John of the Cross, the transcendent Justice, Wisdom and Love responsible (as in Dante's *Inferno* III) for definitively limiting and confining evil to Hell. Eliot's *embrace* – the word is not too strong – of the reality of Hell gives us something like a key to the underlying unity of his various activities after his 1927 conversion and into the 1930s: not just as poet and dramatist, but also as churchman, social commentator and critic.

Before approaching this nexus of activities in light of that embrace it is, however, necessary to explain why the dogma of Hell is prioritized in this account over another idea, more commonplace within Eliot scholarship: that of Original Sin. The clearest account of this concept in Eliot is found in Kenneth Asher's *T. S. Eliot and Ideology*. Asher traces its indubitable influence on the young Eliot first and foremost to Charles Maurras and the Action Française, and later to T. E. Hulme as an English expositor and 'universalizer' of these ideas. Maurras, *the* central figure of French right-wing politics in the early twentieth century, advocated a reversal of the French revolution and a return to an aristocratic, non-democratic society that would be 'classique, monarchique, catholique'. A plank in this ideology was the conception of human beings as corrupt and in need of restraint and systematic discipline by civilizing forces and institutions. Maurras distinguished absolutely between 'the forces of chaos: unbridled emotion, equality, individualism, and revolution', and 'the forces of order: reason, hierarchy, community, and tradition' (Asher 1995: 23). Pitched on the side of chaos were the French revolution and its alleged intellectual progenitor, Jean-Jacques Rousseau. But Rousseau was just one example of a general disintegrative principle of 'romanticism', which Maurras traced back to Luther's Protestant insistence on private judgement, and onwards into the nineteenth-century ideologies of progress, liberalism, democracy and laissez-faire capitalism. Anti-Semitism was also rife within Maurras's organization, with the Jews being portrayed as aliens in France, taking advantage of the French 'collapse' of 1789 to establish a menacing political and financial influence: the Action Française was thus fanatically anti-Dreyfusard.[63] On the side of 'Order' for Maurras was nothing less than the great 'classical' tradition of Western civilization – from its origins in Greece via Rome to the Roman Catholic Church and to Latin Europe and especially France (23). A large part of the appeal of Maurras's perspective for intellectuals was his assimilation of artistic and cultural values such as decorum, restraint, elegance and refined discrimination, which could only truly flourish in a socially stable, hierarchical, traditional society.

However, a peculiarity of Maurras's valuation of the 'catholique' was that he considered the Catholic Church as a neutralizing *check* upon the 'radical anarchism of Jesus' (Asher 1995: 24): 'The merit and honor of Catholicism was to *organize* the idea of God and to remove from it this venom' (Maurras, quoted in Asher 1995: 24). Maurras himself was a non-believer, and politically, for the first time, French Catholics and those of a more sceptical inclination could join together in the Conservative cause. Yet this political advantage had in it the seeds of the movement's later destruction: the Vatican would condemn the Action Française in 1926 precisely for subordinating the Catholic faith to politics.

Asher amply documents the influence of Maurrasian terminology and politics on Eliot, but also notes that it was filtered through T. E. Hulme's less narrowly French formulation of these ideas, focused more sharply upon the idea of Original Sin: 'the conviction that man is by nature bad or limited, and can consequently only accomplish anything by disciplines, ethical, heroic, or political' (Hulme, quoted in Asher 1995: 36). However, Original Sin is not, for either Maurras or Hulme, strictly speaking a *Christian* dogma at all: it has turned into a badge for a certain cultural politics.

On the evidence of the second volume of Eliot's letters (1923–25), there can be no doubt that Eliot conceived his own cultural role as a mediator of this cultural politics in a more subdued, literary form. In a letter to Maurras of October 1923, Eliot tried to enlist the Frenchman as a contributor to the *Criterion*:

> Only *The Criterion* frankly proclaims a philosophy which 'democrassery' is bound to find reactionary, although, in our view, it is the only philosophy which offers the slightest hope of progress at the present time. I am certain that the *Criterion* group represents the body of opinion nearest to l'Action Française.
>
> (Eliot 2009: 238)

As Ronald Bush has emphasized in a review of the letters (Bush 2010: 678–9), Eliot had also written to the *Daily Mail* in January of the same year to compliment the paper on a recent series on Italian Fascism that lauded the 'rescue' of Italy as a 'romance', and as 'one of the most important events of our time' (Eliot 2009: 7). Similarly, in a well-known *Criterion* 'commentary' from April 1924, Eliot praised Hulme as 'the forerunner of a new attitude of mind, which should be the twentieth century mind, if the twentieth century is to have a mind of its own. Hulme is classical, reactionary, and revolutionary; he is the antipodes of the eclectic, tolerant, and democratic mind of the last century' (quoted in Asher 1995: 48).

In Eliot's essay on Baudelaire, there is strong evidence for the continuing relevance of this cultural politics: rejection of the 'progressive degradation' of the nineteenth century with its ideology of Progress, its humanitarianism, its democratic reform, all slot into this picture. And so does the overwhelming sense of *ennui* and despair at the whole condition of nineteenth-century modernity, described as so menacingly insignificant as to make damnation seem a kind of salvation. Furthermore, as is well known, the very terms in which Eliot famously made public his conversion in *For Lancelot Andrewes* (1928) – 'classicist in literature, royalist in politics, and anglo-catholic in religion' – echo the Maurrasian credo.

Nevertheless, two crucial differences mark a separation between Eliot and Maurras: the first present from the beginning, and the second increasingly dominant in Eliot's thought across the 1930s. The former may be indicated by Eliot's praise of a 'decadent' modern poet, Baudelaire, whose style was very far from the decorum and restraint demanded by the Maurrasian line (see Asher 1995: 25–8).

Indeed, Eliot's own experimental poetry, and the work of a whole generation of writers he praised and promoted, seems at odds with Maurras's ideals in this respect. By no stretch of the imagination, for instance, could *The Waste Land* be described as 'classicist' in Maurras's sense; indeed, if romanticism is 'disintegrative', what better example of this tendency than such chaotic, palimpsestic form? However, as critics have long realized, the poem can also be read as being about a world *crying out for* order and regeneration, its juxtaposed fragments of broken civilization, ritual and myth strictly orchestrated to this end, and the whole an illustration of the 'mythical method' that can survey and perhaps re-organize 'the immense panorama of futility and anarchy which is contemporary history' (Eliot 1975: 107).[64] The latter famous comment from the essay 'Ulysses, Order and Myth' (1923) shows how, both before and after his conversion, Eliot was prepared to defend experimental, hyper-modern writing even if it contained indecency (Joyce) or even blasphemy and outright Satanism (Baudelaire). The important thing was that the writing could be construed as displaying the correct *tendency*. In a less well-known letter to the editor of *The Forum* (16 November 1928), Eliot defended Joyce and D. H. Lawrence against a charge of indecency by Granville Hicks, by arguing that these writers were on the right side of

> a transition, a revolt against the paganism of progress of the nineteenth century, toward a rediscovery of orthodox Christianity. Even 'Freudianism', crude and half-baked as it is, is a blundering step toward the Catholic conception of the human soul. The religious faith which Mr Hicks suggests has been destroyed by 'science' was a faith much better destroyed. Perhaps the most interesting example [...] is the spectacle of the grandson of Thomas Huxley discovering that human nature is fundamentally corrupt. This seems to me a healthy sign.
>
> (Eliot 2013: 320)

Joyce, Lawrence and Aldous Huxley could thus be enlisted as engaged in a beneficial, future-oriented creative destruction, targeting the liberal, bourgeois faith of the nineteenth century as a prelude to the revitalizing rediscovery of Christian orthodoxy.[65]

The question of faith here leads on to the second, more decisive point of difference with Maurras. Eliot's conversion led him to a relentless, uncompromising affirmation of Christian supernaturalism, where faith in the dogma and reality of Hell became a litmus test of orthodoxy.[66] In light of this, his early intellectual influences were also found wanting. Although Eliot defended the Action Française against papal condemnation, he was under no illusion with regard to Maurras's own lack of faith and subordination of Christianity to politics. In fact, Eliot's emphatic supernaturalism should be read as an explicit distancing of his own stance from that of Maurras on this point.[67] The letter to More quoted above thus marks the realignment of Eliot's views. The categories of Classicism versus Romanticism were now viewed as distinctly secondary, along with 'culture' and even 'morals'. It is impossible to overstate the effect on Eliot of the sense of God as utterly transcendent Other, terrifying in His grandeur, glimpsed in 'the dark night and the desert'. Eliot repeatedly claimed to have undergone mystical experiences,[68] and again it is crucial to note that after his conversion, belief in 'dogma' no longer served a political and cultural 'Order'. Instead, it was for him about *access* to divine self-revelation. Eliot ultimately came to see Maurras as a kind of Virgil figure, a virtuous pagan capable of leading him to the Earthly Paradise, but unable to ascend further.[69] It is therefore interesting to glance at the treatment of this very moment in Eliot's Dante essay from 1929, which was dedicated to Maurras: at this point (the close of *Purgatorio* XXVII), Dante is crowned and mitred king and bishop over himself, and Eliot deduces that 'political and ecclesiastical organization are only required because of the imperfections of the human will' (ElSE, 261).

These institutions were necessary, but not an end in themselves: they too would pass away. Eliot's properly Christian dogmatic faith *relativizes everything else*, including his own political preferences, for as he cautioned in *The Idea of a Christian Society* (1939), 'whatever reform we carry out, the result will always be a sordid travesty of what human society should be – though the world is never left wholly without glory' (Eliot 1976: 47). This is not, however, meant to foster any Olympian complacency:

> If this is a world in which I, and the majority of my fellow-beings, live in that perpetual distraction from God which exposes us to the one great peril, that of final and complete alienation from God after death, there is some wrong that I must try to help to put right.
>
> (Eliot 1976: 75)[70]

The aim, then, is a whole culture that walks 'in the daily terror of eternity', a point Eliot made explicitly in one of his contributions to the think-tank *The Moot* in 1938:

My comments have chiefly been concerned with the necessity for safe-guarding Christianity itself, in our enthusiasm for society. And I think we need to remember, in the heat of social zeal, that the point of living is to be found in Death, and that we are concerned as Christians with what happens to us after that. I mean that the fear of Hell is not merely a matter of individual temperament, but is essential for collective Christianity.[71]

One consequence of this fundamental shift in Eliot's thinking may sound peculiar to received opinion: the younger Eliot (often seen as more 'radical', less 'reactionary', than Eliot the convert) was demonstrably *more* sympathetic to movements of the Right (chiefly the Action Française, but also early Italian Fascism) than the consciously Christian Eliot would later become. Post-conversion, Eliot criticizes fascism in the same breath as Communism, for setting itself up as a competitor, an *alternative* 'supernatural faith': this is sheer 'humbug' (Eliot 1928: 282). In a letter to the *Church Times* (30 January 1934), he pointedly raised the question of whether the Christian idea and fascist ideology were compatible, implying a negative answer via quotations from Mussolini on the nobility of war as such; scepticism towards ecclesiastical authority; the state as an absolute; and imperialist aggression. Even more strikingly, in the aforementioned review of a number of books (both laudatory and critical) on fascism from 1928, Eliot offered a guarded defence of Maurras's *bête noire*, democracy:

Now it is manifest that any disparagement of 'democracy' is nowadays well received by nearly every class of men, and any alternative to 'democracy' is watched with great interest. [. . .] I cannot share enthusiastically in this vigorous repudiation of 'democracy'. [. . .] It is one thing to say, what is sadly certain, that democratic government has been watered down to nothing. It is one thing to say, what is equally sad and certain, that from the moment when the suffrage is conceived as a *right* instead of as a privilege and a duty and a responsibility, we are on the way merely to government by an invisible oligarchy instead of government by a visible one. But it is another thing to ridicule the *idea* of democracy. A real democracy is always a restricted democracy, and can only flourish with some limitation by hereditary rights and responsibilities. [. . .] The modern question as popularly put is: 'democracy is dead; what is to replace it?' whereas it should be: 'the frame of democracy has been destroyed, how can we, out of the materials at hand, build a new structure in which democracy can live?'

(Eliot 1928: 287)

In his most considered response to the European crisis, written a few months before the outbreak of war in 1939, Eliot gave his own view of how such a new structure might be constructed upon specifically Christian foundations.

The premise of *The Idea of a Christian Society* is that what is needed is 'not a programme for a party, but a way of life for a people' (Eliot 1976: 14). Statesmen in such a reformed Christian society would be 'confined, by the temper and traditions of the people which they rule, to a Christian framework within which to realize their ambitions', and although they may perform un-Christian acts or be unbelievers themselves, 'they must never attempt to defend their actions on un-Christian principles' (22). The people thus governed would largely express their Christianity in behaviour more or less unconsciously governed by social norms, including customary religious observances, and a traditional code of conduct towards one's neighbour: they should be able to perceive 'how far their lives fall short of Christian ideals', yet their religious and social life should form a whole such that 'the difficulty of behaving as Christians should not impose an intolerable strain' (23). Eliot also envisaged an elite 'Community of Christians', both clerical and lay, of 'intellectual and spiritual superiority' (28), able to offer a continuous critique of society as a whole from firmly held dogmatic principles. Two areas falling under their aegis would be education and economics (a sharp critique of consumerism runs through the book). Finally, the Church itself would speak with definitive authority within this society in matters of dogma, faith and morality, and may be expected to frequently rebuke the state (38).

Within some such system of cultural checks and balances, a non-totalitarian Christian democratic system should be workable. Yet Eliot emphasized that his ideal did not assume any particular form of government: any such identification would be a 'dangerous error' (Eliot 1976: 45), confusing the permanent with the transitory. What he urges throughout the book is that it is not just the totalitarian regimes of Italy, Germany or Russia that ultimately boil down to versions of Paganism or materialism: following Liberal principles to the end (seen as a largely negative loosening of restraint) might lead to 'that which is its own negation: the artificial, mechanized or brutalized control which is a desperate remedy for its chaos' (12).

Eliot attacked what he saw as two inadequate attitudes to the European crisis in Britain: first, the complacent assumption that because the Germans profess a semi-pagan 'national religion', *they*, by contrast, are self-evidently Christians; and second, 'worst of all', the advocacy of Christianity (by the Moral Rearmament movement, but also, one notes, by Maurras) 'not because it is true, but because it might be beneficial' (Eliot 1976: 46). Where Christianity is merely a means to some other end, society as a whole is drifting towards a non-Christian endpoint, and the rhetorical thrust of Eliot's book is intended to wake his readers up to this fact, for if those presently 'neutral' are brought to imagine a future *without* Christianity – keeping totalitarian alternatives vividly in mind – they might recoil from the consequences before it is too late. One might dub Eliot's view 'dogmatic rearmament', for he too aims to tap into the national sense of a failure of moral nerve in England after the Munich appeasement treaty abandoning the Czech Sudetenland to Hitler in 1938. Instead of short-term emotional appeals, however, he advocated educational reform on firmly Christian principles. Ultimately, if an all-pervasive *cultural* change is needed, 'A nation's system of education is much more important than its system of government' (33).

This emphasis on culture naturally returns us to Eliot's activity as poet and critic in the 1930s, and specifically to the relationship between dogma, politics and poetry. In an important article on 'Poetry and Propaganda' (1930), Eliot had taken issue with a loose assertion by A. N. Whitehead that one can gain 'doctrine' from poets about the philosophy of nature. Eliot calls this idea 'dangerous nonsense' (1930: 595) in so far as Whitehead is 'confusing the *persuasive* power of poetry with evidence of truth' (597), for the truth of any doctrine can never rest upon an appeal to poetry. On the other hand, the critic must enter into the individual poetic world as far as possible, and allow a persuasive effect to take place: just as training in the discipline of philosophy is a matter of 'the exercise in assumption or entertaining ideas', so 'we have no contact with poetry unless we can pass in and out freely, among the various worlds of poetic creation' (601–2). Eliot did not deny poetic stature to philosophical materialists like Lucretius or Thomas Hardy, since 'what poetry proves about any philosophy is merely its possibility for being lived' (601); that is, the extent to which 'certain worlds of thought and feeling are *possible*' (602). Nevertheless, there is also a tendency inherent in the critical enterprise to want to

> organize our tastes in various arts into a whole; we aim in the end at a theory of life, or a view of life [...] to terminate our enjoyment of the arts in a philosophy, and our philosophy in a religion – in such a way

that the personal to oneself is fused and completed in the impersonal and general. (599)

In the long run, critical appreciation thus *fuels a desire for doctrine*, and poetry can here provide 'intellectual sanction for feeling, and esthetic sanction for thought' (602).

However, in *After Strange Gods: A Primer of Modern Heresy* (1933), Eliot explicitly chose to adopt a *non*-literary point of view. The stature and persuasiveness of the 'heretical' writers he criticizes was simply assumed, and because any important heresy is 'partly right', they may convey 'an exceptionally acute perception, or profound insight, of some part of the truth' (Eliot 1933: 24). But if 'orthodoxy' really is a higher and more complete standpoint, the orthodox critic should be able to see, more clearly than the author, both the strengths and the limitations of a particular work. To extract the real value of a heretical work, such a critic must also be trained to 'redress the balance, effect the compensation' (25) by applying explicitly orthodox standards *as well as* literary ones: hence the idea of a critical 'primer'. For instance, Eliot points to a certain unreality in contemporary literature, resulting from an inability to convey 'moments of moral and spiritual struggle depending upon spiritual sanctions' (42). This again evokes Eliot's emphasis upon the 'daily terror of eternity', and his remarks at this point swiftly lead on to a critique of Ezra Pound's version of Hell in the *Draft of XXX Cantos*:

It consists (I may have overlooked one or two species) of politicians, profiteers, financiers, newspaper proprietors and their hired men, agents provocateurs, Calvin, St. Clement of Alexandria, the English, vice-crusaders, liars, the stupid, pedants, preachers, those who do not believe in Social Credit, bishops, lady golfers, Fabians, conservatives and imperialists; and all 'those who have set money-lust before the pleasures of the senses'. [...] If you do not distinguish between individual responsibility and circumstances in Hell, between essential evil and social accidents, then the Heaven (if any) implied will be equally trivial and accidental. Mr. Pound's Hell, for all its horrors, is a perfectly comfortable one for the modern mind to contemplate, and disturbing to no one's complacency: it is a Hell for the *other people*, the people we read about in the newspapers, not for oneself and one's friends.

(Eliot 1933: 42–3)

As Eliot would later restate this insight in the 1939 *Idea of a Christian Society*, 'so far as a man sees the need for converting *himself* as well as the World, he is approximating to the religious point of view' (Eliot

1976: 75). By contrast, Pound's Hell lacks both 'dignity' and 'tragedy' because it elides daily moral struggle with sanctioned consequences, and projects all evil onto imaginary, scapegoated others.

Christian critics thus have 'a duty of maintaining consciously certain standards and criteria of criticism over and above those applied by the rest of the world' ('Religion and Literature' (1935), in ElSE, 399). Eliot's cultural and political aims fuse in the desire for 'a literature which should be *un*consciously, rather than deliberately and defiantly, Christian' (392). This whole approach is far from the enforced, public mythology of the contemporary totalitarian 'political religions'. There is instead perhaps a whiff of the lonely desert prophet about Eliot's austere insistence on standards appropriate to 'a way of life for a people' that exists no longer, or not yet. Still, it may be asked, what does it mean for an orthodox Christian writer to be actually working within a culture that is not in fact 'unconsciously Christian'? Is he forced, willy-nilly, to be merely defiant in the face of contemporary ills?

If *The Waste Land* cried out for Order, Eliot's post-conversion literature cries out for the intrusion of the radical Otherness and transcendence of God into history; indeed, into the ever-unsatisfactory medium of language itself. This is perhaps most explicit in *Murder in the Cathedral* (1935), where both the weakness and the strength of the play derive from Eliot's application of this principle. The impersonal thinness of its main character Thomas á Becket stems from the idea that a saint is the creation of God alone: 'the true martyr is he who has become the instrument of God, who has lost his will in the will of God, and who no longer desires anything for himself, not even the glory of being a martyr' (ElCPP, 261). Becket's motivation therefore must be largely negative: to avoid doing 'the right deed for the wrong reason' (258) in order to empty himself of personal ambition. It is up to the Fourth Tempter to voice the dangerous vision that haunts him:

> King is forgotten, when another shall come
> Saint and Martyr rule from the tomb.
> Think, Thomas, think of enemies dismayed,
> Creeping in penance, frightened of a shade (254)

At the same time, the Tempter's words foreshadow the actual obeisance to the Church made by King Henry after Becket's death, restoring proper order to the kingdom: and the Chorus at the end affirm that a great cleansing *has* taken place in Canterbury. The strength of the play is not its characterization, but the depiction of this wrenching public ritual, progressing despite all worldly impediment. The Chorus marks its stages. First, uneasy awareness of undesired change: 'Leave us to perish in quiet'; 'We do not wish anything to happen' (243). Then, just before the murder of Becket, this spiritual sterility changes into a salutary awareness of judgement and, of course, the reality of Hell: 'And behind the Judgement the Void, more horrid than active shapes of hell; / Emptiness, absence, separation from God' (272). Then, after the murder: 'We are soiled with a filth that we cannot clean' (276). And finally: 'We thank thee for thy mercies of blood, for Thy redemption by / blood' (281). Into this progress, however, Eliot inserts a sharp disruption, as the knights speak in contemporary prose, implicating the audience in the murder: 'if you have now arrived at a just subordination of the Church to the welfare of the State, remember that it is we who took the first step [...] if there is any guilt whatever in the matter, you must share it with us' (279). The Knights appear to have won the long-term battle, for in a present-day culture universally 'worm-eaten with Liberalism' (Eliot 1933: 13) it may well seem, in the words of the First Priest following Becket's murder, that 'The Church lies bereft / Alone, desecrated, desolated, and the heathen shall build on the ruins, / Their world without God' (ElCPP, 280). The answer, however, is not mere defiance of the World, but *sacrifice*, the immolation of self that allows God to work: 'For the Church is stronger for this action, / Triumphant in adversity. It is fortified / By persecution: supreme, so long as men will die for it' (280).

Immolation is also the keynote of the wartime poem 'Little Gidding' (1942), where, famously, the German bombers at the height of the Blitz are associated with Pentecostal (and Purgatorial) fire:

> The dove descending breaks the air
> With flame of incandescent terror
> Of which the tongues declare
> The one discharge from sin and error.
> The only hope, or else despair
>   Lies in the choice of pyre or pyre –
>   To be redeemed from fire by fire.

(ElCPP, 196)

The theological-political project advanced in *The Idea of a Christian Society* – jolting Britain into awareness of the need for self-purgation if the totalitarian enemy is to be effectively confronted – still shadows these lines: '[a Christian society] involves, at least, discipline, inconvenience and discomfort: but here as hereafter the alternative to hell is purgatory' (Eliot 1976: 19). Yet at the same time, the initiative does not lie with human beings at all ('Who then devised the torment? Love' (ElCPP, 196)), nor is it within their power to remove the 'intolerable shirt of flame' (196). History, seen *sub specie aeternitatis*, is a 'pattern / Of timeless moments' (197): the moments where God is allowed to intrude. The perspective is relentlessly eschatological, marked by the repeated mantra from Julian of Norwich: 'Sin is Behovely, but / All shall be well, and / All manner of thing shall be well' (195). The way of Christian purgation goes *through* sin and error, as 'the rending pain of re-enactment / Of all that you have done, and been' (194), combines with a sense of the futility and sterility of all words not wrought by the Pentecostal flame ('Every poem an epitaph', 197), to fuel a longing for the 'condition of complete simplicity / (Costing not less than everything)' (198) and for the Dantean blossoming of cleansing fire into mystic rose (198; cf. *Paradiso* XXXI). Here too, finally, the 'religious point of view' for Eliot involves converting oneself as well as the World: in 'Little Gidding', the poetic speaker is cast in the role of sacrificial victim, redeeming the time.

Ezra Pound and the Rottenness of Heresy

Eliot's adherence to a strict orthodox supernaturalism, epitomized by his insistence on the dogma of Hell, led him to a careful separation of Christian faith from politics (conceived as a means to religious ends), literary and cultural criticism (to be informed by dogmatic principles), and the role of poetry and literature (inherently propagandistic and thus never wholly trustworthy, though able to give 'aesthetic sanction' to a worldview by showing what inhabiting it might be like). This patient taxonomy is in stark contrast to Ezra Pound's idiosyncratic blurring of the lines between religious, political and literary 'dogma', between poetic vision and historical reality, between poetry and propaganda, and between perceived cultural 'vitality' and religious belief. Although the focus here is trained upon the 1930s and 1940s, it is worth glancing at an earlier text (from *The New Age*, 13 January 1921) to gain a sense of the development in Pound's thinking about the idea of religious dogma:

AXIOMATA

(1) The intimate essence of the universe is not of the same nature as our own consciousness.

(2) Our own consciousness is incapable of having produced the universe.

(3) God, therefore, exists. That is to say, there is no reason for not applying the term God, *Theos,* to the intimate essence.

(4) The universe exists. By exists we mean normally: is perceptible to our consciousness or deducible by human reason from data perceptible to our consciousness.

(5) Concerning the intimate essence of the universe we are utterly ignorant. We have no proof that this God, Theos, is one, or is many, or is divisible or indivisible, or is an ordered hierarchy culminating, or not culminating, in a unity.

(6) Not only is our consciousness, or any concentration or coagulation of such consciousness or consciousnesses, incapable of having produced the universe, it is incapable of accounting for how said universe has been and is.

(7) Dogma is bluff based upon ignorance. (EPSP, 49)

It is somewhat startling to compare this text with the following quotation from an unpublished 1940 article draft: 'I have been asked whether I am a Catholic and I am not ready to deny it. I don't expect any organization to accept responsibility for my speculations. I do not 13th March anno XVIII deny any Catholic dogma' (Pound 1996b: 141). Given his earlier opinion, Pound's 'non-denial' of Catholic dogma is surprising; papal infallibility, for instance, would hardly go well with points five, six and seven of the 'Axiomata'. Furthermore, Pound had also dated the end of the 'Christian era' to 'midnight of the 29–30 October (1921)',[72] and in 1932 would start reckoning a new era from the 1922 Fascist March on Rome, rather than from the birth of Christ – a reckoning he still used until the fall of Fascism in 1945. Pound actively supported Mussolini, at least from their meeting in June 1933 until the ignominious end of the Salò Republic in 1945; after which he was arrested and nearly tried for treason by his native USA on account of his many radio broadcasts in support of the wartime Axis. In this light, it should not be too much of a surprise that Pound did not undergo conversion to the Catholic Church. However, he did gradually change his position on the usefulness of some

Catholic dogma for his own thinking: chief among them the medieval condemnation of *usury*. According to Pound, the stage when that injunction began to be more weakly enforced was when the slow rot of Western civilization set in, indeed 'the Catholic Church rotted when its hierarchy ceased to believe its own dogma' (EPGK, 164). Pound also came to believe that the Mediterranean Roman Church should be considered the historical bearer, and possibly part of the future, of what he called the European religion.

The Pound of 1921, then, produces a list of paradoxically anti-dogmatic 'axiomata'. Pound's apodictic statements are designed to clear away conceptual obstacles to the reception of visionary experience: 'The theos may affect and may have affected the consciousness of individuals, but the consciousness is incapable of knowing why this occurs, or even in what manner it occurs, or whether it be the *theos*' (EPSP, 50). 'Mysticism' is one result of this state of affairs, but mystical 'visions or auditions or sensations' such as 'Dante's Rose or Theresa's walnut' (50) do not carry any *evidential* value capable of setting them apart from other intense experiences – 'the taste of a lemon or the fragrance of violets or the aroma of dung-hills' (50) – whether sensual or intellectual or artistic. Pound did not acknowledge any strict boundaries between the spiritual and the material: almost anything could for him become a means to vital, live, epiphanic communication with the 'intimate essence of the universe', even if such contact could never be reduced to codified knowledge. The Greek myths, for example, are 'explications of mood', the record of 'delightful psychic experience'; this experience, not the record per se, has a 'permanent basis in humanity'.[73] The creative artist is thus the figure par excellence who channels these vital energies, in ever-changing forms, at various times in history. Correspondingly, the artist for Pound was a prototype for 'constructive' activity generally, whether in thought, learning, literature, art, science, economics or politics. The avant-garde artist or 'constructor' was instinctively able to grasp the 'Paideuma', a term Pound had adapted from the German ethnologist Leo Frobenius to mean 'the active element in the era, the complex of ideas which is in a given time germinal, reaching into the next epoch, but conditioning actively all the thought and action of its own time' (254). In his own time, Pound anticipated and sought to give birth to a vast cultural shift, a second Renaissance.[74] It is central to this whole picture that the 'theos' *must not* be pinned down, fixed, dogmatically defined: to do so is to calcify and dampen artistic-constructive creativity and fluidity: 'Belief is a cramp, a paralysis, an atrophy of the mind in certain positions' (49).

Yet here we find the roots of Pound's own dogmatic strain, evident throughout his career: the obstacles to the vision and the mysteries, and to 'constructive' activity in history and society, are to be attacked, condemned, blasted, lacerated, cut away like a cancer. Suddenly, from an unexpected angle, we are close to the medieval sense of heresy as a corrupting force, eating at morals and societal cohesion from the inside. As Pound wrote to John Lackay Brown in April 1937 (Pound 1950: 293), 'The Protestant world has *lost* the sense of mental and spiritual *rottenness*. Dante has it: "gran sacco che fa merda." The real theologians *knew* it.' The reference[75] is to *Inferno*, Canto XXVIII (25–7), where the sowers of discord, in this case Mohammed, are themselves physically split open, exposing their corrupt insides to plain sight: '*l tristo sacco | che merda fa di quel che si trangugia*' ('the miserable sack | that makes of what we swallow excrement').

By 1937, Pound had long since identified the source of rottenness and evil throughout Western history: *usury*. Pound's economic obsessions began after his meeting with Major C. H. Douglas in 1918, effected through their common friend A. R. Orage, the editor of *The New Age*, the little magazine where Douglas's 'Social Credit' theory was first published and promulgated alongside Pound's prose.[76] Douglas argued that the meaning of money itself should be revised to mean the 'credit' of the community: stemming from the common cultural inheritance of production methods and technology, plus an assessment of the potential for future production. Money should not be correlated with existing wealth and goods or measured in gold, but should instead function purely as a means of exchange and the fair distribution of purchasing power: a 'ticket' giving access to goods and services. To this end, a citizen's wage or 'national dividend' should be established; money should circulate rather than be hoarded; and the state, not the banks, should control credit and adjust prices. Pound later advocated payment of the dividend and other social benefits through Silvio Gesell's Stamp Scrip system, designed to make money circulate by gradually reducing the value of the monthly bills issued. He also mapped these theories onto the fascist idea of the state by arguing that, under totalitarian central control, credit could more easily be dispensed by the state rather than by banks.

Pound's analysis also became increasingly conspiratorial: banks and financiers, by charging interest for credit and so producing money 'out of nothing', were unfairly imposing debt upon the community as a whole, and the system perpetuated itself because of their vested economic interest. Pound's technical definition of usury was 'A charge for the use of purchasing power, levied without regard to production; often without regard to the possibilities of production' (EPCan, 230). However, his interest in these matters was far from purely technical. Pound increasingly saw the so-called 'usuriocracy' as a secret cabal corrupting history, not least through their supposed responsibility for arms dealing and hence war – especially the Great War of 1914–18. And he increasingly associated this group with the Jews, who came under vicious attack from Pound from about 1936. For Pound, the economic crises of the 1930s proved that liberal democracies were nothing more than tools of the usuriocracy, whereas some version of social credit could potentially cure unemployment and poverty.

In Pound's admiration for Mussolini, the paradox of a supposedly anti-dogmatic artist embracing totalitarianism and the cult of the Leader is amplified to fever pitch. The gap was bridged for Pound by his notorious definition of Mussolini as an artist-politician:[77]

> I don't believe any estimate of Mussolini will be valid unless it *starts* from his passion for construction. Treat him as *artifex* and all the details fall into place. Take him as anything save the artist and you will get muddled with contradictions. Or you will waste a lot of time finding that he don't fit your particular preconceptions or your particular theories.
>
> (Pound 1970b: 33–4)

Mussolini is seen precisely as an overthrower of preconceptions and established theories – the fixed, the formulaic – for the sake of fluid, vital, 'artistic' improvisation: 'The DUCE sits in Rome calling five hundred bluffs (or thereabouts) every morning' (35); Pound's honorary title for him would be 'MUSSOLINI DEBUNKER' (35). Pound fantasized that investing all power in such a Leader could enable practical debunking specifically of the 'usuriocracy' – although, as Tim Redman has pointed out, until the advent of the Salò Republic at least, there were few signs that Mussolini intended to adopt the economic policies favoured by Pound. But Mussolini was not simply the hammer of usurers in Pound's conception: he would also 'remagnetize the will' of Italy (95); foster new learning and 'AWAK-ENED INTELLIGENCE' (73); achieve a national unity of purpose and 'order' that would restore 'civilization' (108); and also instigate a reli-gious renewal based on the implicitly syncretistic or even pagan 'Mediterranean sanity' (31) that essentially left the means of achiev-ing contact with the *theos* to the individual's choice. I will return to this point, but it is here worth noting again how Pound's dogmatism continued to present itself as necessary for preserving or fostering an anti-dogmatic syncretism.

So much, then, for a brief sketch of some economic and political motivations behind Pound's preoccupation with usury: but a glance at the famous 'Usura' Canto (LXV), written in 1935, expands the issue beyond the political situation of the 1930s, and leads us back to Pound's approval of the disgust with 'spiritual rottenness' found in the medieval theologians and Dante. It is important to hear the sheer *wildness* of Pound's accusations: clearly, much more is at stake for the poet than it could be if 'usury' were merely understood in the limited sense of the formal definition that follows the poem ('charge for the use of purchasing power . . . ', EPCan, 230).

> With usura hath no man a house of good stone
> each block cut smooth and well fitting [. . .]
>
> with usura, sin against nature,
> is thy bread ever more of stale rags
> is thy bread dry as paper,
> with no mountain wheat, no strong flour [. . .]
>
> wool comes not to market
> sheep bringeth no gain with usura
> Usura is a murrain, usura
> blunteth the needle in the maid's hand
> and stoppeth the spinner's cunning. [. . .]
>
> Usura slayeth the child in the womb
> It stayeth the young man's courting
> It hath brought palsey to bed, lyeth
> between the young bride and her bridegroom
>
> CONTRA NATURAM (EPCan, 229–30)

It is important to note that Pound did in fact think of this poem partly in contemporary political terms: in two letters to Oswald Mosley from 1938 and 1939 he insisted that it should be actively used in propaganda for the British Union of Fascists,[78] and Pound himself read it out on the air in one of his 1942 radio broadcasts, emphasizing in his introduction how the Canto is 'plumb AGAINST usura' and 'indicates certain consequences that will result so long as you have it, and in measure as it is all pervasive'.[79] Yet these 'consequences' seem far from obvious, unless one realizes that Pound is precisely attempting to revive and channel the medieval condemnation of this heresy.[80] A medieval world of sound craftsmanship ('house of good stone', 'spinner's cunning') and farming ('strong flour', wool) is evoked in contradistinction to a decadent modernity in which things are made to 'sell and sell quickly' (EPCan, 229), and the touchstone of cultural achievement is Trecento and Quattrocento Italy:

> Pietro Lombardo
> came not by usura
> Duccio came not by usura
> nor Pier della Francesca; Zuan Bellin' not by usura
> nor was La Callunia painted.
> Came not by usura Angelico; came not Ambrogio Praedis,
> No church of cut stone signed: Adamo me fecit.
>
> (EPCan, 229–30)

The medieval understanding of usury is best summed up by Thomas Aquinas:

> To take usury for money lent is unjust in itself, because this is to sell what does not exist. [. . .] In order to make this evident, we must observe that there are certain things the use of which consists in their consumption: thus we consume wine when we use it for drink and we consume wheat when we use it for food. [. . . W]hoever is granted the use of the thing, is granted the thing itself and for this reason, to lend things of this kind is to transfer the ownership. Accordingly if a man wanted to sell wine separately from the use of the wine, he would be selling the same thing twice [. . .] Now money, according to the Philosopher (Ethic. v, 5; Polit. i, 3) was invented chiefly for the purpose of exchange: and consequently the proper and principal use of money is its consumption [. . .].[81]

Pound's prophetic capitals CONTRA NATURAM must be understood in light of the argument that usury corrupts the natural use and consumption of the fruits of the earth (wine, wheat), and is also against the nature of money itself, being a means of exchange only.

Furthermore, in Diana Wood's summary of the tradition, if money is stored through a loan, 'it will neither increase nor diminish, which is another way of stating that it is sterile: barren money cannot breed' (Wood 2004: 161). Thus, as Pound was fond of pointing out: 'In theology, as Dante knew it, the usurer is damned with the sodomite. Usury judged with sodomy as "contrary to natural increase", contrary to the nature of live things (animal and vegetable) to multiply' (EPSP, 61). Hence the extravagant monstrosity of Pound's Usura, slaying the child in the womb and infecting the bridal bed with palsy. His hyperbole makes little sense except against the large metaphysical canvas of medieval economic thought, which considered usury as 'theft of time, which was owned by God alone for the common benefit of mankind' and saw it as worse than the one-off crimes of robbery or even murder since 'a loan never sleeps, but always grows' (Wood 2004: 164). The Council of Lyons in 1274 condemned 'the canker of usury which devours souls and exhausts resources' (quoted in Wood 2004: 163); at this point usury had long been classed as a mortal sin, and it was decreed that manifest usurers were excommunicate and unfit to be buried in consecrated ground.

However, a dogmatic council of the Latin Church proceeds on the assumption that it possesses the authority to accurately interpret and define the revealed law of God, whereas it was Pound's axiomatic conviction that no one possessed the authority to formulate anything at all about the will or the inner nature of 'the theos'. Pound squared this circle by maintaining that the Roman Catholic Church, at its best, had served in medieval times as a vehicle for the survival of just the kind of non-dogmatic ancient paganism (chiefly the 'Eleusinian mysteries') favoured by Pound himself. Moreover, the Church supposedly declined in vitality and cultural importance when it started to dilute its condemnation of usury whilst imposing dogmatic sanctions on the thinkers and writers (such as Scotus Eriguena and the Provençal poets) of whom Pound approved. Yet the institution might again become a useful tool for the regeneration of what Pound called the 'European religion' – but only if properly purged of all 'semitic infections', including the monotheistic presumption of unique access to divine law. Pound's ingenious reasoning here is worth tracing more fully.

In *A Light from Eleusis* (1979) and *The Birth of Modernism* (1993), Leon Surette charts Pound's highly speculative construction of an alternative, heretical tradition lodged within Latin Christianity – one that reached its cultural high-point in the Provençal troubadours and Italian *stilnovisti* poets like Guido Cavalcanti. Under the heading *Credo*, Pound summed up his long-standing conviction thus in 1930: 'I believe that a light from Eleusis persisted through the middle ages and set beauty in the song of Provence and of Italy' (EPSP, 53). The mysteries at Eleusis honoured the goddess of harvest and fertility, Demeter, who searched for her daughter Persephone, dragged into the underworld by the god Hades. The earth is barren in those months of the year when Persephone is with Hades, but when she returns, Demeter restores fertility. The mysteries dramatized the descent of Persephone and her return to Demeter. The rites are not known in detail due to the secretive nature of the cult, but have been thought to culminate in a ritual marriage perhaps involving coition. Pound tended to poetically amalgamate Demeter with Venus/Aphrodite (Surette 1979: 48–9). For him, these figures were emblems of the inter-connected sacredness of the natural growth-cycle and human sexuality, and adherence to their 'mysteries' (whether in the Eleusinian festivals, or later May Day rituals, or the poetics of Lady-worship and *Amor*) came to demarcate a kind of private orthodoxy for Pound. For opposed to this sensibility is the 'incorrect doctrine' of 'corpse-worship and the worship of Atys':[82]

> By 1934 Frazer is sufficiently digested for us to know that opposing systems of European morality go back to the opposed temperaments of those who thought copulation was good for the crops, and the opposed faction who thought it was bad for the crops (the scarcity economists of pre-history). [...] The Christian might at least decide whether he is for Adonis or Atys, or whether he is Mediterranean. The exact use of dyeing Europe with a mythology elucubrated to explain the thoroughly undesirable climate of Arabia Petraea is in some reaches obscure.[83]

A synopsis of Frazer's *Golden Bough*, chs 29–36, is needed to unpack Pound's meaning here. Briefly, Frazer argues that the vegetation deities of Egypt and Eastern Asia (Pound's 'Arabia Petrea') – variously called Osiris, Tammuz, Adonis and Attis – were behind many Christian rituals. One example is the Greek tradition of displaying a wax effigy of the dead Christ on Good Friday, which is fervently kissed and later solemnly buried, after which there is lamentation and a strict fast until midnight on Saturday; similarly, the ceremonies of both Tammuz and Adonis were associated with effigies of the dead corn-god, whereas the priests of Attis practised self-castration in some places. Pound is arguing that there is an unhealthy strain of 'corpse-worship' and self-castrating asceticism within Christianity, as opposed to the sounder 'Mediterranean' (or 'European') survivals of the Eleusinian fertility cult. He further associated this ascetic strain with a law-bound, iconoclastic monotheism stemming from the Hebrew scriptures – one re-emphasized during the Reformation by Martin Luther and John Calvin – thus all things life-denying and prohibitionist could be located in the 'Semitic' Near East, as an alien intrusion into authentic European culture.

While Pound had, at an earlier stage of his career, tended simply to use this narrative to attack all forms of Christianity, his interest in 'usury' led him towards a reassessment of the role of the Roman Catholic Church – in Italy in particular – from about 1936 and into the war years. To be sure, this alignment was in no small measure strategic, as Pound systematically set about building alliances with individuals within the Church whom he perceived as sympathetic to his economic policies, such as the notoriously anti-Semitic radio priest Father Charles Coughlin, or Archbishop Pietro Pisani, who according to Leon Surette got Pound published in the *Osservatore Romano* and sent him a 'rattling good book' on the medieval doctrine of the 'just price'.[84] As Surette points out, Pound also marketed the Catholic Church to the Douglasites in a 1936 review called 'The Church of Rome', where he claimed that 'there is to my mind a profound agreement between Douglas and the canonists' (quoted in Surette 1999: 272). Writing to Douglas himself (25 February 1936), Pound claimed that 'The CHURCH can back up our MORALS/ anything we do inside the VOCABULARY of the Church can be APPROVED; Get that?' (quoted in Surette 1999: 272). It is interesting and paradoxical to see him, in this period, lashing out at the editors of *The Neo-Christian* (a New York journal advocating a 'universal religion' beyond sectarianism) with an assertion seeming more spontaneous than strategic: 'The teaching of the Catholic Church is CLEAR. Any man who refuses to examine the teaching of that Church on USURY is a coward, and I doubt his honesty, mental or spiritual.'[85] Still, in the very same 1940 text in which Pound claims not to deny any Catholic dogma, there is this outburst: 'The Church, servant of Rothschild, is certainly not a Christian organization, the lackey and pet boy of usuriocracy is not a religion, it is a bordello and not clean as a bordello' (Pound 1996b: 141). Still later, after the war, Pound would revert to his hostility against all 'Christers'.[86]

Nonetheless, Pound's motivation for his 1930s rapprochement with the Church is not solely determined by contemporary politics: he was also elaborating a dogmatic defence of the idiosyncratic poetic faith he had been constructing for most of his career; a faith he eventually dubs the true religion of Europe. Once upon a time, and especially in thirteenth- and fourteenth-century Italy, the Roman Church opposed all usury as contrary to natural increase; fostered many ritual practices stretching back to the worship of Demeter and Aphrodite; and erected churches such as the Tempio Malatestiano at Rimini that were alive with this syncretistic religious feeling, decorated by superb artists and craftsmen, mediating contact with the Theos through evoking a 'painted paradise' upon the church wall. In the Polish classicist Thaddeus Zielinski's book *La Sybille* (1924), Pound found support for the view that the true 'Old Testament' of Christianity was the religion of pagan Greece, and *not* the Hebrew scriptures: concepts like the Trinity, or the cult of Mary and the Saints, could never, Zielinski argued, have been acceptable to monotheistic Judaism, but were rather received by the already-pagan Gentiles (see Surette 1999: 270–1). At its height, the Roman Church could thus be tolerant of the Neo-Platonic speculations of a Scotus Eriugena (*c*.815–77) arguing that 'all things are lights',[87] and, later, tolerant of the Lady-worship of the troubadours, supposedly rooted in the Eleusinian cult. This, for Pound, was a Church that had true authority, one that, in Pound's favourite Eriugenean phrase, stemmed from 'right reason, never the other way on'.[88] Its anathemas (such as those at the Council of Lyons mentioned before) were thus worthy of respect: they spoke of confidence and cultural vitality. In this way, Pound was conveniently able to claim the dogmatic support of the Catholic Church at the height of its cultural prestige, even while denying any permanence to the authority of the Church-as-institution; all the while insisting upon the *non*-dogmatism of his own poetic faith, as opposed to the strictures derived from Hebrew monotheism. The proper context for his 1940 'non-denial' of Catholic dogma, then, is this whole historical mythology, which allows Pound to have his dogmas and disown them, too.

For Pound, however, the Church fell from this height of cultural achievement, which had been a time when 'the Church authorities BELIEVED what they were taught or were still searching for the truth', a period when 'Europe's best intellect and intelligence was IN the Church' ('Ecclesiastical History', EPSP, 61). This fall was due to a dilution of the teaching on usury – to the point where the rise of banking was allowed, and a 'banker pope', Leo X, would eventually try to charge 'ALL possible taxes' to build St Peter's (62). While Leo dismissed Luther's 'crude theology', the German cleric was successful because he hitched it onto an 'economic grievance' (62), namely the sale of indulgences. An important turning point, in Pound's reading, was the 'scandal of the Albigensian crusade' (61) in his beloved Provençe. For Pound, this military campaign was the first major suppression of the vibrant counter-tradition of Neo-Platonist occultism and the Eleusinian mysteries that he himself favoured. From this war arose the Inquisition, and there followed a time when the Church 'no longer had faith ENOUGH to believe that with proper instruction and argument the unbeliever or heretic could be made to see daylight. Invocation of authority to MAKE him believe' (61). The Church's authority is, then, appropriate and healthy when blasting usury with full force; whereas coercive authority is supposedly only exercised later, to shore up a waning confidence. By extension, Pound's own attacks on the '*rottenness* of heresy' may have invoked the authority of the medieval theologians and the Roman Church at the height of its powers, but this did not – of course – make of *him* an authoritarian Inquisitor.

Pound's 1934 article on 'Ecclesiastical History' quoted throughout the previous paragraph was the sixth of his instalments in a debate with T. S. Eliot over *After Strange Gods*, which Pound had reviewed for the *New English Weekly*. This was a debate in which the two contestants were talking entirely past each other, a spectacle which illustrates how very different were their views on the *function* of dogma. To Eliot, as we have seen, faith in the Church's dogma promised access to supernatural reality. Without Hell, Heaven and a transcendent God, the moral life of humanity seemed to him a pointless game. Eliot's critique of Pound's version of Hell (abode of usurers) in the Cantos was that it lacked the tragedy and dignity deriving from that divine sanction. Contrariwise, the best one could hope for would be a mere *painted* Paradise, wherein, through 'a redistribution of purchasing power, combined with a devotion, on the part of an élite, to Art, the world will be as good as anyone could require' (Eliot 1933: 42). Whereas this for Eliot is still unreal, 'vaporous' (42), for Pound, there *is* (axiomatically) no other access to contact with 'the theos' than through intense experience. All the rest is 'bluff based upon ignorance'. Correctly understood, 'benevolent dogma' can, in Pound's view (in 'Axiomata', EPSP, 49), practically safeguard and foster such experience within a historical culture, but it cannot account for, describe or validate those experiences. They are ends in themselves.

On the other hand, 'malevolent dogma' (49) imposes rigid formulae on experience, thereby devitalizing it, and Pound's constant accusation against 'the Possum' was that he was playing dead, embracing dead-letter rules, corpse worship, asceticism and a 'lot of dead cod about a dead God' (EPGK, 301).

Their respective schemes for *re*-vitalizing European culture in the face of the 1930s crisis therefore naturally look quite different: for Eliot, a new Christendom that would dispel modern *ennui* by embracing the daily terror of eternity; for Pound, the rebirth of 'European religion':

> We want an European religion. Christianity is verminous with semitic infections. What we really believe is the pre-Christian element which Christianity has not stamped out. The only Christian festivals having any vitality are welded to sun festivals, the spring solstice, the Corpus and St. John's eve, registering the turn of the sun, the crying of 'Ligo' in Lithuania, the people rushing down into the sea in Rapallo on Easter morning, the gardens of Adonis carried to Church on the Thursday.[89]

Whenever Pound expounds his religion – as in the following quote from an unpublished article entitled 'European Paideuma', intended for a pro-Nazi propaganda journal in 1939 – the issue of dogma, and the dividing line between orthodox and heretic, is never far away:

> Again I assert that there is one disease that one can stigmatize as utterly unEuropean. The European does NOT get hold of an idiotic text, proclaim it infallible and authoritative and then proceed to explain it, to give it meanings extraneous to its verbal formulation, and worship it. This plague and infection is from the near east. [...] Instead of calling the European non-religious one wd/ do better to say that he backs his instinct against an obviously tricky or foolish text. Searching for truth he sees no need to hamstring himself with a formula which may or may not have been constructed in the course of honest search for a difficult verity.[90]

Pound's target here is obviously the Hebrew Old Testament, and it is worth noting that the last two pieces were written less than a year after the 1938 Italian race laws and the German *Kristallnacht*, on the cusp of war. In the course of the previous few years, Pound's anti-Jewish rhetoric ('verminous', 'infection', 'plague') had increasingly come to resemble that of German Nazis. While originally critical of Hitler before the formation of the Axis in 1936, Pound supported him from the late 1930s and into the war, increasingly via his many propaganda broadcasts for Rome Radio.[91] Indeed, even after the Führer's death, Pound, detained on charges of treason, insisted that he had been 'a saint'.[92] It seems clear that the idiosyncratic 'European religion' expounded by Pound overlaps in a number of ways with the pagan revivalisms featuring within the political religions of both Fascist Italy and Nazi Germany. To be sure, a study is needed of how the symbolism employed in these *nationalist* movements (such as the grain imagery in Italian Fascism)[93] was absorbed and reworked by Pound into a scheme for revolutionary *European* 'rebirth'. In the present context, though, it is notable that Pound's construction of his European Paideuma allowed him to maintain that the real dogmatism, the real authoritarianism – the real totalitarianism, in fact – is always that of the enemy.

After the Axis defeat and under arrest, writing from the American Detention Center in Pisa, Pound found himself evoking the authority of the Church and of Christian history once again, albeit from a different angle: 'I believe in the resurrection of Italy quia impossibile est' (Canto LXXIV, EPCan, 462). The 'resurrection of Italy' clearly refers to the whole of Pound's political and poetic-religious faith: the driving force of the last 15-odd years of his life. All is ruin: Mussolini is dead and 'twice crucified' (EPCan, 445), first deposed in July 1943 and then killed in Milan in April 1945. Europe was overrun. How to believe in that resurrection now? Pound's use of Tertullian's phrase *quia impossibile est* has been glossed somewhat carelessly in Carroll F. Terrell's *Companion* to the *Cantos*, as 'From Tertullian: "Credo qui impossibile"' (1993: 381), a wording not found in the ancient writer but based rather on the popular myth of Tertullian as an irrationalist and a fideist advocating belief in the impossible, or even the absurd ('Credo quia absurdum est' being another corrupt variant).[94] The correct wording is to be found in *De Carne Christi*, V.4:

> *Et mortuus est dei filius; credibile est quia ineptum est.*
> [The Son of God died: it is immediately credible – because it is silly.]
> *Et sepultus resurrexit; certum est quia impossibile.*
> [He was buried, and rose again: it is certain because it is impossible.][95]

Tertullian is arguing against the Docetist Marcion, who denied that Christ had a real body, and correspondingly thought the flesh shameful. Tertullian's point was that Christians could never even have begun holding such very extraordinary convictions unless they were derived from fact and experience: their apparent silliness or impossibility thus constitutes indirect proof of their credibility. It is certain *because* it appears 'impossible'. Behind Tertullian's rhetoric is, in turn, this famous passage from St Paul's first letter to the Corinthians (1:23–5):

> But we preach Christ crucified, unto the Jews a stumblingblock, and unto the Greeks foolishness; But unto them which are called, both Jews and Greeks, Christ the power of God, and the wisdom of God. Because the foolishness of God is wiser than men; and the weakness of God is stronger than men.

Pound's *quia impossibile est* seeks to channel poetically this flamboyant Christian defiance of merely conventional, superficial 'wisdom': apparent weakness and defeat may yet be a prelude to a resurrected ideal polis, 'now in the mind indestructible' (EPCan, 462). A letter to Olivia Rossetti Agresti shows that Pound still clung to this thought eight years after the war: 'AND when someone starts gathering honest men / they may have an Italy. quia impossibile est.'[96] In Eliot's postconversion literature, I have noted a sustained prayer for God's intervention into history from without. In Pisa, Pound's *credo* is even more naked and threadbare, miming its defiance with purloined rhetoric. This poet cannot appeal to Almighty God, but must finally direct his petition to the historic process itself.

W. H. Auden: The Would-Be Christian

The rise of Nazism and the onset of war was a key factor in W. H. Auden's gradual rediscovery of Christian faith about 1939–40. In particular, seeing a newsreel in early December 1939 on the conquest of Poland – cheered on by attending German residents in Manhattan with shouts of 'kill the Poles' – shook Auden into a fundamental consideration of the values by which his own civilization claimed to exist.[97] As he later summarized it, even the Communists had claimed to believe, with liberalism, in *some* version of the universal brotherhood of man and neighbourly love, but

> The novelty and shock of the Nazis was that they made no pretense of believing in justice and liberty for all, and attacked Christianity on the grounds that to love one's neighbour as oneself was a command

fit only for effeminate weaklings, not for the 'healthy blood of the master race'. Moreover, this utter denial of everything liberalism had ever stood for was arousing wild enthusiasm [...] in one of the most highly educated countries in Europe [...]. Confronted by such a phenomenon, it was impossible any longer to believe that the values of liberal humanism were self-evident. Unless one was prepared to take a relativist view that all values are a matter of personal taste, one could hardly avoid asking the question: 'If, as I am convinced, the Nazis are wrong and we are right, what is it that validates our values and invalidates theirs?'

(APr III, 578)

In contemporary essays and reviews from 1939 and into the war, this dilemma is frequently reinvestigated: 'For the past hundred years Occidental liberalism has lain snug in the belief that the relation of its arts and sciences, of its ethical and political values, to the Christian faith was simply historical. It has taken Hitler to show us that liberalism is not self-supporting' (APr II, 131). Like Eliot, Auden saw liberalism's value system as ultimately dependent upon the legacy of Christianity. Furthermore, like Eliot he saw the challenge of Hitler precisely in making this fact so evident that it called for a basic stand on the future of the civilization that had emerged from Christianity. However, Auden did not share Eliot's wish to re-establish Christendom via the cultural activism of well-educated guardians of orthodoxy: instead, he sought out new theological ideas that might ground liberal democracy more firmly by reconnecting it with its Christian roots, while still shunning claims to be 'in possession of the final truth' (APr II, 10). The latter phrase, from a *pre*-conversion review published in March 1939, forms part of an accusation that Fascism and Catholicism, while seemingly at odds, are united in this claim to possession of the Truth. By contrast, the 'first principle of democracy, on the other hand, is that no one knows the final truth about anything' (10); there can be only partial and particular 'approximation' to it (10). One aim of Auden's theological speculation was to secure and revitalize liberal democracy itself, most notably by pointing to how such approximations do still relate to a transcendent Absolute, and how brotherly love must finally be infused with Christian *agape* to become effective and convincing. Thus for Auden, the 'special revelation' on which Christianity's 'real claim to supremacy is founded' (APr II, 133) is that most paradoxical of doctrines, the Incarnation, where the Word is made Flesh (John 1:14), and Christ enters *into* our frail and limited condition, taking 'upon him the form of a servant [...]

made in the likeness of men' (Philippians 2:7). Both in his occasional essays from the war years and in the long Christmas oratorio *For the Time Being*, written 1941–42, Auden explored what exactly a commitment to this doctrine might mean in his own time, while consciously guarding against what he calls 'the way of dogmatic belief backed by force' (APr II, 29).

Auden was able to bridge the gap between recommending faith in Christian dogma, on the one hand, while maintaining that no one is in possession of final truth on the other, via his concept of the 'would-be Christian' (APr II, 163):[98]

> There is no such thing as a Christian or a Christian society for no one can say: 'I am a Christian', only 'I am a sinner who believes that Jesus is the Christ whom I am required to become like. I shall not be a Christian or even understand fully what the word Christian means until I have become like him.'
>
> (APr II, 193)

As Edward Mendelson explains, Auden's reading of Søren Kierkegaard (from March 1940 onwards) was fundamental to his theological outlook. A key phrase for Auden was Kierkegaard's 'Before God I am always in the wrong.' 'Kierkegaard's existential Christianity offered two strengths that psychoanalysis and politics could not: it perceived its relation to an absolute value; and it understood that it could never claim to know or embody that value' (Mendelson 1999: 130). As Auden would put it in a 1944 review of Kierkegaard's *Either/Or*, 'the existential philosopher begins with man's immediate experience as a *subject*, i.e. a being in *need*, an *interested* being whose existence is at stake.' Therefore, what Kierkegaard teaches is 'an approach to oneself, not a conclusion, a style of questioning to apply to all one's experience' (APr II, 213–18; quoted in Mendelson 1999: 131). Neediness and imperfection are of course universal, and the only way for someone to communicate to a fellow human being 'why he believes Jesus to be the Christ' (APr II, 196) would be through suggesting that Christ uniquely appeals to and challenges this common predicament. Thus, while it is true that the would-be Christian 'cannot believe this without meaning that all who believe otherwise are in error, yet at the same time he can give a no more objective answer than the lover', namely, 'I believe because He fulfills none of my dreams, because He is in every respect the opposite of what He would be if I could have made Him in my own image' (196–7). Embracing Christ's love here means to subject oneself to a constant moral and intellectual self-examination: it is a style of questioning placing the whole of one's existence at stake. The act of trying-to-believe Christian dogma in order to become like Christ is not an abandonment, but an intensification of such questioning: 'for it is as difficult to be orthodox, i.e. not merely recite but fully assent to all the articles, as it is to be humble or chaste' (250). Auden continues:

> A heresy is an attempt to make God in one's own image; that is why there have to be so many different ones, to suit each person's idea of himself. The sanguine man finds the Incarnation easy to believe but is offended at the Cross; the choleric man is attracted by the heroism of the Cross, but repelled by the command to turn the other cheek; the melancholic man finds Original Sin an obvious truth, but the forgiveness of sins a difficult mystery. (250)

From Auden's perspective, therefore, his kind of Christianity was profoundly in keeping with democratic procedure, since 'Protestantism, like democracy, is based upon the assumption that controversy is a form of cooperation, and ultimately the only way of arriving at truth' (APr II, 86). However, cooperation required an active and engaged citizenry, and assumed that 'the average man is sufficiently energetic and interested in truth to take his part in looking for it' (86). In an earlier review called 'Democracy is Hard', for instance, Auden argued that democracy cannot be 'sustained or defended unless one believes that pride, lying, and violence are mortal sins, and that their commission entails one's damnation' (28). Democratic procedures need to be supported by individual spiritual practice: 'Frankly, democracy will only work if as individuals we lead good lives, and we shall only do that if we have faith that it is possible and at the same time an acute awareness of how weak and corrupt we are' (29). The principles of self-examination and fallibility here become the basis for an extraordinary anti-totalitarian *credo* that blends democracy, Agape and the scientific method:

> There is one way to true knowledge and only one, a praxis which, if defined in terms of human relations, we should call love. For what is the scientific attitude but that of the love which does not reject the humblest fact, resists not evil (recalcitrant evidence) nor judges, but is patient, believing all things, hoping all things, enduring all things? And what is its opposite but the way of dogmatic belief backed by force? Skepticism, then, in belief. Absolute faith in the way and in the existence of truth. (28–9)

Like Eliot, Auden stressed the anti-romantic theme of 'original sin' (APr II, 99) and humanity's 'natural bias toward evil' (98). Yet Auden's account of the political implications deriving from this stance amounted to a determined revision of the reactionary emphasis on Order, Hierarchy and Monarchy that Eliot inherited from Maurras and Hulme:[99]

> No individual or class, therefore, however superior in intellect or character to the rest, can claim an absolute right to impose its view of the good upon them. Government must be democratic, the people must have a right to make their own mistakes and to suffer for them, because no one is free from error. (98)

This emphasis on error and sin confronted in fear and trembling nevertheless represents only one half of Auden's theological (and political) vision. A decisive influence on Auden's theological thought was the British writer Charles Williams, whose *The Descent of the Dove: A Short History of the Holy Spirit in the Church* was instrumental in his return to faith. Auden first read it in February 1940, and (as Mendelson 1999: 124–7 points out) immediately began incorporating phrases from Williams into the final lines of the long poem he was writing, *The New Year Letter*. He also lifted his title for the overall collection, *The Double Man*, from Williams. Mendelson's account of this extensive borrowing is excellent, but the profounder impact of Williams's highly original understanding of Incarnation arguably only becomes fully evident in Auden's next long poem, *For the Time Being* (begun October 1941 and finished in July 1942). At this point, he had also read the first volume of the American theologian Reinhold Niebuhr's *The Nature and Destiny of Man*. Auden's review of that book from June 1941 shows that Incarnation was very much on his mind: as Ursula Niebuhr noticed, Auden was here promoting a relatively peripheral theme in her husband's work to great prominence. A combined account of these two writers on Incarnation will supply the background for a look at *For the Time Being* itself.[100]

The distinctive and idiosyncratic term 'co-inherence' echoes across Charles Williams's condensed history of the church.[101] By taking on human nature, Christ enters into an intimate, *substitutional* exchange with his creatures:

> 'God was in Christ, reconciling the world to himself . . . and hath committed unto us the word of reconciliation.' 'He hath made him to be sin for

us, who knew no sin; that we might be made the righteousness of God in him' – 'an exceeding and eternal weight of glory'. In such [scriptural] words there was defined the new state of being, a state of redemption, of co-inherence, made actual by that divine substitution, 'He in us and we in him.'

(Williams 1939: 8–9)

Williams, though an Anglican, accordingly approved of the Catholic idea of intercession by the saints, for 'the exchanges of Christendom are very deep; if we thrive by the force of the saints, they too may feed on our felicities' (32).[102] More generally, co-inherence involved bearing one another's burdens in this life. Williams extensively quotes an unnamed desert monk on this point:

It is right for a man to take up the burden for them who are near to him [...] to put his own soul in the place of that of his neighbour, and to become, if it were possible, a double man, and he must suffer, and weep, and mourn with him [...] as if he had acquired his countenance and soul, and he must suffer for him as he would for himself. For thus it is written *We are all one body*. (55)

Here, then, is a vision of a mystical – yet still emphatically corporeal – community of sacrificial *agape*, which affected Auden immediately upon encountering it. In fact, one of many Williams quotes in Auden's *New Year Letter* is the phrase 'Our life and death are with our neighbour' (Mendelson 1999: 126).[103] Auden's understanding of democracy as a community constructed from the condition of universal and original sin ('true democracy begins / With free confession of our sins')[104] is thus profoundly rooted in Williams's analysis of 'co-inherence':

The co-inherence reaches back to the beginning as it stretches on to the end, and the *anthropos* is present everywhere. 'As in Adam all die, even so in Christ shall all be made alive'; co-inherence did not begin with Christianity; all that happened then was that co-inherence itself was redeemed and revealed by the very redemption as a supernatural principle as well as a natural. We were made sin in Adam but Christ was made sin for us and we in him were taken out of sin. *To refuse the ancient heritage of guilt is to cut ourselves off from mankind as certainly as to refuse the new principle.*

(Williams 1939: 69–70, my italics)

The heritage of guilt *connects* us all through co-inherence; and that heritage can itself only be fully revealed and apprehended in the light of Christ's Incarnation and redemption. We cannot fully know what it means that we were 'made sin in Adam' until we fully know that 'Christ was made sin for us and we in him were taken out of sin': a lifetime's task for the would-be Christian. In his review of Niebuhr's *Nature and Destiny of Man*, Auden focuses upon how the 'more important significance of the Incarnation' (APr II, 133) is not, in Niebuhr's words,

> the finiteness of man but of his sin, not his involvement in the flux of nature but his abortive efforts to escape that flux. The issue of Biblical religion is not primarily the problem of how finite man can know God but how sinful man is to be reconciled to God and how history is to overcome the tragic consequences of its false eternals [...] The content of the revelation is *an act of reconciliation in which the sin of man becomes the more sharply revealed by the knowledge that God himself is the victim of man's sin and pride.* Nevertheless the final word is not one of judgement but of mercy and forgiveness.
>
> (Niebuhr 1964: 147, quoted in APr II, 133, my italics)

Here, too, the visions of Incarnation and original sin mutually interpret each other. For Auden, the most 'brilliant' chapters in Niebuhr are those dealing with the Christian conception of sin, wherein Niebuhr derives sin from 'the fact that man refuses to admit his "creatureliness"; he pretends to be more than he is' (APr II, 133). But in the Incarnation, Christ himself freely assumes this very condition, 'at an actual moment in historical time, the Word was actually made flesh, the possibility of the union of the finite with the infinite made a fact' (133). Overreaching and pretence and escape will no longer do, and 'only faith in the Incarnation can conquer man's original anxiety' (134). Acknowledging human 'creatureliness', and thereby our sin, is the only means of access to Christ's glorification of that same creatureliness; but also to the *agape*-community that this creates on earth, 'that invisible coinherence of souls in the love of Christ which is the Church Catholic and Universal' (APr II, 172). For Auden, startlingly, a fully revitalized democracy would ultimately need to be modelled on the Church.

In *For the Time Being*, it is the 'Meditation of Simeon' that most explicitly sets out the incarnational theology at the heart of Auden's Christmas Oratorio:

The Word could not be made Flesh until men had reached a state of absolute contradiction between clarity and despair in which they would have no choice but either to accept absolutely or to reject absolutely [...].

(ACP, 387)

But here and now the Word which is implicit in the Beginning and in the End is become immediately explicit, and that which hitherto we could only fear as the incomprehensible I AM, henceforth we may actively love with comprehension that THOU ART.

(ACP, 387–8)

And because of His visitation, we may no longer desire God as if He were lacking: our redemption is no longer a question of pursuit but of surrender to Him who is always and everywhere present. Therefore at every moment we pray that, following Him, we may depart from our anxiety into His peace.

(ACP, 390)

The dramatic tension explored across this text is between an anxious state of 'absolute contradiction between clarity and despair' and the necessary surrender to His peace. Auden's technique is to manipulate a continuous parallel between the historical moment of Incarnation (using the iconic reference-points of the Annunciation, the Nativity, and the Flight into Egypt) and those predicaments large and small, contemporary and perennial, which the Incarnation addresses and redeems by substitution and co-inherence. Simeon's speeches setting out the preconditions for the Incarnation therefore have a double reference, to what needed to happen in history before Christ could appear *and* to what still needs to be repeated in the minds of the present generation: 'Before the Unconditional could manifest Itself under the conditions of existence, it was necessary that man should first have reached the ultimate frontier of consciousness, the secular limit of memory beyond which there remained but one thing for him to know, his Original Sin' (ACP, 387). As Auden revealingly wrote to his father, 'I was trying to treat it as a religious event which recurs every time it is accepted' (quoted in Mendelson 1999: 186).

The backdrop for Incarnation in Auden's wartime play, then, is an ominous atmosphere of conflict, and of spiritual desert, applicable both to ancient Palestine and *Anno Domini* 1941:[105] 'The evil and armed draw near / The weather smells of their hate' (ACP, 350) – 'no nightmare / Of hostile objects could be as terrible as this Void' (352) – 'For the garden is the only place there is, but you will not find it / Until you have looked for it everywhere and found nowhere / that is not a desert' (353). Yet a counterpoint impulse of prayer and praise also emerges from within this near despair:

> Though written by Thy children with
>   A smudged and crooked line,
> Thy Word is ever legible,
> Thy meaning unequivocal,
>   And for Thy Goodness even sin
> Is valid as a sign. (374)

Whereas Auden had used the word 'crooked' in his 1937 poem 'As I Walked Out One Evening' ('You shall love your crooked neighbour / With your crooked heart' (ACP, 135)), its homosexual slang undertone[106] survives into *For the Time Being* with a key difference. Where the former poem stresses unconquerable Time and indelible earthly imperfection, in the latter crookedness and even sin are capable of divine inscription. Homosexuality is presented here as but one type of human 'crookedness', and Auden's oratorio is immensely inventive in cataloguing the sheer multiplicity of spiritual conditions that the Incarnation must address and enter into in order to truly make the Word legible to all.

Thus, the three wise men need redemption from their intellectual vices: science as (Baconian) 'inquisition' of nature; the (Bergsonian) philosophy of time-as-flow; or a (Platonic) ethical idealism of the pure Ought and the Greatest Good, which 'left no time for affection' (ACP, 369). The 'shepherds', for Auden 'the poor and humble of this world for whom at this moment the historical expression is the city-proletariat',[107] are tempted to despair by the sense of being mere pegs in an inhuman machine: they are shown the joy of existence as arbitrary gift, as they rush toward Bethlehem. More sinister is the figure of Herod, who congratulates himself on the civic improvements made in his reign ('Allotment gardening has become popular . . . Things are beginning to take shape' (391)) and boasts of his ability to uphold Rational Life and Civilization as against the 'incoherent wilderness of rage and terror' (391) outside the Empire. Yet incomprehensibly, his subjects want more than sweet reasonableness, a 'wild prayer of longing' (392) still rises up everywhere, and one day Herod is confronted with three men who say God has been born. This dangerous rumour must be stamped out, 'Civilisation must be saved even if it means sending for the military' (394). Even if true, the idea of a God-Man would still be *intolerable*, since it would raise a transcendent ethical standard which finite humanity could not attain – inducing 'madness and despair' (394). Herod's whole philosophy is that the overwhelming terror and incoherence 'outside' can only be fought piecemeal, while the limited civilized order is always under threat. The new vision of a universal, radical divine love that transcends and upends this picture therefore endangers that effort and vigilance. Thus Herod, and with him contemporary liberalism, is finally impaled on the paradox of having to uphold the status quo – namely 'the most impersonal, the most mechanical and the most unequal civilisation the world has ever seen' (APr II, 6) – by violence, despite officially benign intentions: 'I've tried to be good . . . I'm a liberal. I want everyone to be happy' (ACP, 394). The Incarnation thus introduces a wholly different political vision:

> As the new-born Word
> Declares that the old
> Authoritarian
> Constraint is replaced
> By His Covenant,
> And a city based
> On love and consent
> Suggested to men,
> All, all, all of them.
> Run to Bethlehem. (378)

Gathered around the Christ child, Joseph and Mary epitomize this new Covenant, and, as such, they are called upon to bear the burdens of others. As Mendelson notes, the section called 'The Temptation of St. Joseph' portrays Joseph's doubts about Mary's virginity, as well as his jealousy, which channelled Auden's intense experience of betrayal by his lover Chester Kallmann. Auden had had to face 'the infinite vileness of masculine conceit',[108] to the point of nursing, and briefly enacting, a desire to kill Chester. Joseph's task is to atone for all masculine conceit through the ages:

> For his insistence on a nurse,
> All service, breast, and lap, for giving Fate
> Feminine gender to make girls believe
> That they can save him, you must now atone,
> Joseph in silence and alone

> (ACP, 364)

He must accept, with 'female' passivity, the interruption of the Child into the natural order without any male contribution: 'To choose what is difficult all one's days / As if it were easy, that is faith. Joseph, praise' (365). In the section called 'At the Manger' (379–80), Mary, for her part, must suffer the realization that her very 'mother love', her 'watchfulness', may only tempt the Christ child away from the Father's will: 'What have you learned from the womb that bore you / But an anxiety your Father cannot feel?' Her courageous prayer to the child therefore is: 'Escape from my care: what can you discover / From my tender look but how to be afraid?'[109] From the beginning, Mary must be prepared to offer her protective love itself as a sacrifice: 'O have you / Chosen already what death must be your own? / How soon will you start on the Sorrowful Way?' Her offering of even this most human of loves thus partakes in Christ's offering of all human attachments to the Father: 'Yet not my will but yours be done' (Luke 22:24).

The epilogue of *For the Time Being* returns us to the desert, first through the Holy Family's flight into Egypt ('Fly from our death with our new life' (ACP, 398)), and finally to a contemporary scene of post-Christmas holiday *tristesse*, with the tree being dismantled and cold reflection revealing how one has 'attempted – quite unsuccessfully – / To love all of our relatives, and in general / Grossly overestimated our powers' (399). The exalted perspective of Incarnation 'where for once in our lives / Everything became a You and nothing was an It' is already fading, and 'We look round for something, no matter what, to inhibit / Our self-reflection' (400). With Lent and Good Friday looming, it is the noontime of *acedia*, 'When the Spirit must practice his scales of rejoicing / Without even a hostile audience' (400). Yet 'rejoicing' remains a duty even so, in the midst of war but also in the more ordinary run of things: 'Seek Him in the Kingdom of Anxiety; / You will come to a great city that has expected your return for years' (400).

Lucy McDiarmid presents an important but flawed reading of the poem's conclusion: 'Distancing himself from a Christmas that was constructed of holly and tinsel and mistletoe, the Narrator explicitly dissociates literature and spectacle from spiritual value. Here the Narrator speaks like Puck or Feste, undoing the fiction of the play in the *plaudit*' (McDiarmid 1990: 92). Accordingly, for McDiarmid, Auden's 'poem literally deconstructs itself, puts its pieces into cardboard boxes', and its central philosophical point is the 'concession of its own significance to an extrapoetic God' (92). Her reading usefully emphasizes the wider anti-totalitarian strain in Auden's poetics, its resistance to any notion 'that poetry could and ought to provide absolutes' (10). Auden's distancing devices prevent the poetry from becoming propaganda by displaying its own artifice, its tinsel. Still, McDiarmid's emphasis on an anti-poetic disavowal pointing to an exclusively 'extrapoetic' significance seems overstated and overly iconoclastic, since the Incarnation in For the Time Being is actually said to redeem the Imagination itself, precisely 'from promiscuous fornication with her own images' (ACP, 388). McDiarmid fails to take account of Auden's specifically Incarnational[110] 'theory of art from the standpoint of the Christian faith' (APr II, 163). This theory is first mooted in a March 1941 essay on Joyce and Wagner, evident in For the Time Being, but finally set out at length in his 'Lecture Notes' for The Commonweal from November 1942.

Auden thus argued that Christianity had a revolutionary effect on the subject matter of art. Unlike the pagans – who 'thought that the Good Life was relatively easy for the nobly-born and impossible to the low-born' (APr II, 117) – the Christian vision of original sin is democratic, for now 'any character or situation was artistically interesting that could show spiritual growth or decay' (117). The mundane and the ordinary consequently grows full of significance – even the 'tea-table' (117), which, in For the Time Being, becomes 'a battlefield littered with old catastrophes' (ACP, 389). The return to the everyday world at the close of Auden's oratorio indicates that *even here* the Incarnation can and must work through co-inherence – just as Joseph must 'atone' for the most trivial forms of masculine conceit (the bar-fly, the aggressive scribble on the toilet wall). Similarly, within Auden's theory there is, in art as in all human activity, an element of sin; namely, the 'sin of idolatry' (APr II, 169). Yet this does not mean that art is so hopelessly flawed that it can only constantly disavow itself, for 'art is redeemed when its function is redefined as, not the expression or communication of emotion, but the becoming conscious of emotion' (167). To be sure, art is not 'a magic for arousing proper emotions' (166), nor should it serve 'a consciously political function' (167); instead, the artist's task is to 'find out what his feelings are, and, of course, most of these will be neither pleasant nor good' (167). Within a Christian framework these feelings are interesting enough to matter spiritually, and artworks may induce similar self-exploration in others, uniting an audience not out of mass emotion but 'because they share the same knowledge of weakness, and dare not therefore judge each other' (167). Auden's conclusion here recalls the invocation to 'Seek Him in the Kingdom of Anxiety' at the end of *For the Time Being*: 'Art cannot make a man want to become good, but it can prevent him from imagining that he already is; it cannot give him faith in God, but it can show him his despair' (167). *Pace* McDiarmid, this is a kind of spiritual value – however much it remains the case for Auden that 'only faith in the Incarnation can conquer man's original anxiety' (134).

Conclusion: Modernism and Christian Dogma

Scepticism over dogma, and Christian dogma in particular, is often understood as a defining feature of literary Modernism. Pound's 'Axiomata' might, upon first sight, provide a paradigm for such a view: our consciousness is 'incapable of accounting for how said universe has been and is', while dogma is 'bluff based upon ignorance'. However, Leon Surette has pointed to the real danger of a historical confusion here, for 'at the time [M]odernism was being born, Nietzscheanism, Marxism, positivism, and occultism all perceived Christianity as a common antagonist' (1993: 93–4); and again, 'there is a confusing overlap between Jacobins, utilitarians, aesthetes, occultists, Poundians, Nietzscheans, and Marxists. All are hostile to Christianity simply because it represents the status quo' (78). In other words, these and other positions may be superficially lumped together as 'anti-dogmatic' largely because of their shared antagonism to Christianity (itself motivated, of course, in a variety of ways). Yet each of these groups would – naturally enough – be 'sceptical' only in some cases, while insisting upon their own axiomata in others. For Pound, these included his own privileged access to 'the intimate essence of the universe' or 'Theos' through aesthetic experience; he also believed in an incoherent 'secret history'[111] about the survival of a distinct set of occult beliefs and pagan rites through Western history. Further, he believed he had identified 'usury' as the chief agent of evil throughout history, and that it needed to be blasted with the same dogmatic force as the Church once did. This soon led to anti-Semitic conspiracy theories, and he ended up believing he had correctly identified the politics of the future 'Paideuma' in Mussolini's Fascism and to a lesser extent in Hitler's Nazism. The Christian poets, meanwhile, could claim their own kind of 'scepticism'. Both Eliot and Auden saw human beings as deeply flawed through original sin: weak, imperfect, ill-equipped to know God or themselves, and in need of salvation from self-inflicted anxiety and *ennui*. From this angle, Pound's belief in his own privileged insight might easily evoke the sin of pride.

'Scepticism', then, is much too imprecise a term to contain what is at stake in an often simultaneously 'dogmatic' and 'anti-dogmatic' Modernism. It may be more appropriate to speak of a crisis of authority, a term able to make room for both Christian and non-Christian Modernists. For what is to count as an authentic source of authority in a world of radically clashing worldviews? Who or what is heretical? What is to count as the moribund, the degenerate, the merely traditional, the passé? Christianity? Liberalism? Fascism? Socialism? How, exactly, does one 'make it new'? Which fresh theory, or which updated model from the past, holds the key to the future? Can civilization be renewed through human agency, and if so, what would count as cultural vitality and strength? What words, what literary forms, are trustworthy, and what, if anything, distinguishes poetry from propaganda?

A closer look at this last question reveals how these three poets' relationship to dogma is in fact at the heart of their respective conceptions of their art. Without doubt, the poet most willing to employ his own work for explicit propaganda purposes was Pound. Paradoxically, this attitude was connected with his high valuation of poetry as a medium giving access to unique, privileged insight. For Pound, the best poetry stood in opposition to everything formulaic and moribund: it destroys such shackles in order to connect poet and reader with a quasi-divine vital energy, which could map and synthesize whatever ideas were currently shaping the emergent 'Paideuma'. Figures in philosophy, politics or economics of whom Pound approved were described in terms associated with poetry and art: thus Mussolini is both 'constructor' and 'artifex'. As Jeffrey Perl has noted, 'Pound accepted much of what the fascists did in early years on the assumption that Mussolini would end up following his régime's leading poet into a new renaissance' (1984: 261). For Pound, the artist is *avant-garde* in every sense:

> The artist [...] is always too far ahead of any revolution, or reaction, or counter-revolution, or counter-reaction for his vote to have any immediate result; and no party programme ever contains enough of his programme to give him the least satisfaction. The party that follows him wins; and the speed with which they set about it, is the measure of their practical capacity and intelligence.[112]

Pound was quite open about the fact that he was writing propaganda in the 1930s: 'I am not writing Italian propaganda, any more than I am

writing British propaganda. I am, if you like, writing European propaganda for the sake of a decent Europe wherein the best people will
not be murdered for the monetary profit of the lowest and rottenest'
(EPPer, VII, 33). This of course restates his obsessive concerns: usury
and the propagation of the political faith of fascism as the basis for
a new 'European Paideuma' with its European religion. The aims and
methods of Pound's poetry, the prose and the radio broadcasts are, in
this respect, continuous. Pound's Modernist 'ideogrammic' method
of juxtaposing significant fragments from history and thought, sometimes providing quite minimal context for the reader, was intended to
force his audience to work out for themselves the complex, live-wire
connections he was trying to convey, thus inducing an 'epiphanic'[113]
experience that could foreshadow political conversion. Pound was
constantly propagating this faith, and it bears remembering here that
the term 'propaganda' first became current after the 1622 establishment of the Catholic *Sacra Congregatio de Propaganda Fide*.[114] However,
Pound's insistence upon speaking from deep within his own tangle of
ideas, with few concessions to his audience, made much of his work
singularly ineffective as 'propaganda' in the derogatory sense of a sim-
plified, one-dimensional, emotional appeal to the masses. Instead,
Pound may have been directing his appeal chiefly towards other elites
and artist-constructors; those 'best people' capable of the kind of
epiphany and conversion his work insistently demands.[115] In doing
so, Pound even attempted to borrow the dogmatic authority of the
Catholic Church: in his hectic alliance-building and writerly activity in the 1930s and 1940s, he was implicitly trying to build an elite
'church' around his own doctrines, one that could shape the course
of history.

By contrast the two Christian poets, Eliot and Auden, were deeply
suspicious of claims to any privileged insight for poetry as such,
and also suspicious of poetry's capability for persuasive emotional
rhetoric. The problem is at least as old as Plato's dismissal of the poets
from the republic. Yet it is given an emphatically Modernist, crisis-of-
authority edge by 1930s totalitarianism: *anyone* can claim such insight,
and anyone can make use of such suasion, however mistaken or
harmful the doctrine. Nonetheless, both Eliot and Auden rejected
the Platonic answer – itself reminiscent of totalitarian practice – that
poets must either be exiled or forced simply to teach correct doctrine in their poetry. They never proposed that poetry should simply
teach Christian dogma or fall silent: on the contrary, their respective

Christian theories of literature were carefully designed to validate a full range of expression, including formal experimentalism, heresy and even blasphemy. These specifically Christian frameworks could both assess the value and shortcomings of other literature, while at the same time attributing some form of spiritual significance to their own poetry. For Eliot, as we have seen, heretical writers may convey acute insights, although in the absence of a moral and spiritual struggle depending upon real supernatural sanctions, they remain incomplete. It is 'dangerous nonsense' to confuse the persuasive power of poetry with evidence of truth. Poetry is, among other things, a particular kind of exercise in entertaining ideas: as such, it can only show how a certain worldview is capable of being lived. Here, though, is a role for Eliot's own poetry: informed by Christian doctrine, it is nonetheless the record of a fierce and emotionally tense attempt to 'wrestle / With words and meanings' (ElCPP, 179) that interweaves 'intellectual sanction for feeling, and esthetic sanction for thought' (Eliot 1930: 602).

For Auden, Christianity introduced a new interest in the ordinary and mundane spiritual struggle. All human stories *matter*, and from a Christian standpoint all attempts to become conscious of emotions (good or bad) through art are of interest. All art may commit the sin of idolatry by drawing attention to itself rather than God, but rightly understood, this only reminds readers of our common weakness, thus preparing the ground for Incarnational faith. Auden's wartime poetry, therefore, is full of these self-conscious reminders. Again it is clear that dogma is a key heuristic tool for all three writers: as a focal point for their philosophies, as a mode of reflection on their own art and as a spur to new writing.

In the 1930s, the Modernist crisis of authority is considerably sharpened by the growth of totalitarianism, and by more general critiques of liberalism, democracy and the capitalist economy. As argued at the beginning of this chapter, this provoked a widespread examination of what the fundamental values and character of 'Western civilization' had been and should be, and for many the political crisis could not easily be separated from a religious one. How was Europe's Christian past to be understood, and was a post-Christian future unfolding? In this situation, all three poets examined here became interested in Christian dogma as a way of connecting them to that past in vital and indispensable ways, while at the same time adapting their understanding of such dogmas to present-day tensions that they sought to resolve in their own work. Eliot presents the clearest case here, in his persistent exploration of the movement from modern *ennui* to faith in supernatural judgement. His embrace of the doctrine of Hell and the necessity for purgation as a literary, cultural and political tonic does not only look backwards, but also forwards to a fully revitalized Christendom. For Auden, liberal democracy itself needed to be reconnected with its Christian roots and given a transcendent purpose beyond maintenance of the status quo. To do so, Auden appropriated Charles Williams and Reinhold Niebuhr on Incarnation, and exercised his considerable theological imagination in order to construct a stance that could be both non-totalitarian and potentially salvific. Finally, even Pound's hostility to Christianity cooled temporarily when he began to see the revival of a resistance to 'usury' as a possible basis for political collaboration with the Catholic Church, with the Church itself becoming a vehicle for the re-establishment of the 'European religion' that had supposedly flourished in the thirteenth and fourteenth centuries. Each poet, then, reflected intensely upon what the very notion of holding a dogma has meant and might mean; and in each case, we find evidence of considerable artistic reinvention and appropriation of ancient Christian dogmas to a new crisis. For these Modernists, such reflection became a creative vehicle for confronting the pressing problem of authority anew, and never simply a retreat from complexity into predefined, unchallenging formulas.

4

SAMUEL BECKETT, MODERNISM AND CHRISTIANITY

> For my part, it is the *gran rifiuto* that interests me, not the heroic
> wrigglings to which we owe this splendid thing.
> – Samuel Beckett, letter to Georges Duthuit,
> 9 March 1949 (SBL2, 140)

Christianity is Samuel Beckett's fundamental antagonist: his thought,
his aesthetics and his writing cannot be fully understood in isolation from his lifelong struggle with it.[116] That may seem a large
claim, until one realizes how persistently Beckett returns to this *agon*
with Christianity when defining his whole artistic project vis-à-vis
those of his contemporaries and chosen precursors. A telling emblem
of this is the above letter to Duthuit (part of an important series
from 1949 which culminated in the publication of *Three Dialogues with
Georges Duthuit* in December). Inserted into the discussion of Bram
Van Velde's painting is a reference to the 'great refusal' made by one
in Dante's zone of unnamed neutrals in *Inferno* III, those rejected by
both Heaven and Hell and driven to chase one banner after another
for eternity. In *Three Dialogues*, Van Velde's art is tellingly associated with Beckett's own obsessive concern with a 'fidelity to failure'
(SBDi, 145); similarly, in another letter, Van Velde exemplifies 'fidelity
to the prison-house, this refusal of any probationary freedom' (to
Duthuit, 2 March 1949; SBL2, 130). The artistic task of the *gran rifiuto*
therefore is to remain within a probationless zone of rejection and
expulsion, tracing the ever-onward but futile movement inside the

prison-house of existence, while eschewing both heroism and any kind of redemption. Characteristically, both in the Duthuit letters and in *Three Dialogues*, Beckett associates the attempt to shrink from this task (to 'recuperate'[117] failure), with Christian imagery: 'a Pietà with a double virgin mother' (Beckett to Duthuit, 9 March 1949; SBL2, 141), 'the bosom of Saint Luke' (SBDi, 143). This trend stretches back to his first monograph, where Beckett takes Proust to task for imagining that some residual Romantic transcendence can be achieved through involuntary memory; this merely reveals an anxiety to be a 'good and faithful servant' (Matthew 25:23; SBPD, 81). Beckett is testily aware of the drive towards any and all forms of replacement religion, not least within Modernism, and his persistent reaction is to suggest that this is in fact hardly to stray from Christianity at all. This gives unique weight to Beckett's reaction to (and against) Christianity, and to the terms he draws from Christian tradition – such as the *gran rifiuto* itself. The purpose of this chapter is thus to examine what may be dubbed Beckett's *reductio ad Christianum* across four areas that are central to both Beckett and a range of other Modernist writers: the problem of theodicy, the influence of Dante, the attractions of mysticism and the rhetoric of Apocalypse.

Beckett against Theodicy

After reading Arthur Schopenhauer in 1930, Beckett embraced what he called the philosopher's 'intellectual justification of unhappiness',[118] and shortly began using Schopenhauer's system as a template for his exegesis of Proust. Schopenhauer's ethical disgust at metaphysical optimism became for Beckett a stick with which to beat Christianity:

> For the rest, I cannot here withhold the statement that *optimism*, where it is not merely the thoughtless talk of those who harbour nothing but words under their shallow foreheads, seems to me to be not merely an absurd, but also a really *wicked*, way of thinking, a bitter mockery of the unspeakable sufferings of mankind.
>
> (Schopenhauer 1969: 326)

The optimist party may be best represented by Alexander Pope's classic statement of the eighteenth-century theodicy of 'universal harmony' in *Essay on Man* (1734):

> All Nature is but Art, unknown to thee;
> All Chance, Direction, which thou canst not see;
> All Discord, harmony not understood;
> All partial Evil, Universal Good.[119]

By contrast, in Schopenhauer's analysis nature is a projection screen for the Will as noumenon or thing-in-itself, which, within the phenomenal world, is ever at war with itself. The individuated will strives blindly and endlessly, and every temporary satisfaction either entails immediate transition to another desire (hence privation, suffering) or an interval of empty longing, *ennui*.[120] Adapting this framework, Beckett argued that Proust's characters are 'victims and prisoners' of Time (SBPD, 12–13), driven by an insatiable 'thirst for possession' (15) of objects of desire which, however, are inherently in flux and ungraspable. Beckett also made Schopenhauer's conclusion on tragedy his own: 'what the hero atones for is not his own particular sins, but original sin, in other words, the guilt of existence itself' (Schopenhauer 1969: 254). This becomes a familiar refrain: most explicitly in *Proust* ('the sin of having been born' (SBPD, 67)), in *The Unnamable* ('a punishment for having been born perhaps' (SBT, 312)) and acknowledged as a staple theme in *A Piece of Monologue* ('Birth was the death of him. Again' (SBCD, 425)). The juxtaposition of metaphysical optimism and 'unspeakable sufferings' in order to underline the 'wickedness' of such optimism is a recurring literary strategy for Beckett: a clear instance here would be Winnie in *Happy Days*, buried to the neck in sand in scorching heat yet praising 'Another heavenly day', 'Hail, holy light' (SBCD, 138, 160). A pointed example directed explicitly at Christian redemption is the poem 'Ooftish' (1938), which according to James Knowlson relates to a sermon Beckett heard in 1926 on visiting the sick, arguing that 'the crucifixion is only the beginning. You must contribute to the kitty' (Knowlson 1997: 67). The poem plays sardonically with this idea:

> cancer angina it's all one to us
> cough up your T.B. don't be stingy [...]
> we'll make sense of it we'll put it in the pot with the rest
> it all boils down to blood of lamb.

> (SBPo, 59)

This idea that 'making sense' of suffering through Christ's sacrifice amounts to an almost obscene act of 'boiling down', in a foul blend of disease and 'blood of lamb', provides a clue to much crucifixion

imagery elsewhere in Beckett. The emphasis is on a *universal* crucifixion, which 'the' crucifixion cannot redeem.[121] Hence for instance
the Two Thieves motif, with the middle figure of Christ reduced to
a rotting tooth set in the decaying flesh of Sucky Moll in *Malone
Dies*; or simply absent in *Waiting for Godot*, where both character
pairs may compare themselves to Christ, yet his word of judgement
or salvation fails to arrive. Beckett's distrust of redemptive schemes
eventually encompassed even Schopenhauer's own system: the idea
of a final 'abolition' and transcendence of individual willing and entry
into a Nirvana-esque Nothingness (Schopenhauer 1969: 411–12) was
only one more attempt at reaching for a 'solution', or 'way out'.[122]
On Beckett's reading, Schopenhauer fails to maintain fidelity to his
own prison-house vision of being by reinstating Heaven: this is to
abandon the zone of rejection and the *gran rifiuto*.

Beckett extends his resistance to Christian redemption – as
paradigmatic of all forms of redemption – further than any other
contemporary writer. This is best seen against the background of
other reactions against the eighteenth-century theodicy of universal
harmony. The most influential statement of that theodicy in English
is undoubtedly William Paley's *Natural Theology* (1802). Paley finds
an immense complexity of design everywhere in nature, and in his
chapter on 'The Goodness of the Deity' tries to prove that such design
is beneficial and providential. What may appear evil is actually a
necessary component of a larger good: 'Of *mortal* diseases the great
use is to reconcile us to death. The horror of death proves the value
of life [...] *Death* itself, as a mode of removal and of succession, is
so connected with the whole order of our animal world, that almost
every thing in that world must be changed, to be able to do without
it' (Paley 2008: 259). Charles Darwin, at one time an ardent admirer
of Paley at Cambridge, sums up the nineteenth-century disillusion-
ment with this view: 'I cannot persuade myself that a beneficent and
omnipotent God would have designedly created the Ichneumonidae
with the express intention of their feeding within the living bodies of Caterpillars, or that a cat should play with mice.'[123] In *Watt*
(SBW, 132–3), Beckett joins this critique with characteristically savage
irony:

> But our particular friends were the rats, that dwelt by the stream ... we
> would sit down in the midst of them, and give them to eat, out of our
> hands, a nice fat frog, or a baby thrush. Or seizing suddenly a plump
> young rat, resting in our bosom after its repast, we would feed it to its

mother, or its father, or its brother, or its sister, or to some less fortunate relative.

It was on such occasions, we agreed, after an exchange of views, that we came nearest to God.

Of course, Beckett was not alone in attacking the idea of the Paleyan designer-God as 'a spiteful, narrow, wicked, personal God, who was always interfering and doing stupid things – often cruel things'. The latter quotation comes from Bernard Shaw's lay sermon *The New Theology* (1907), which pilloried the 'old theology' of an omnipotent and beneficent Creator. Instead, Shaw advocated a theology of the Life Force, where 'god' is not omnipotent but is an evolutionary drive to produce something higher: conscious man, and beyond that, the Nietzschean 'superman'. This amounts to what the historian of religion James C. Livingston has called 'the transformation of theodicy to *anthropodicy*' (Livingston 2007: 71): the justification of the ways of God by the emergence of man. It will not be surprising by now that Beckett also attacked such 'anthropomorphic insolence' (SBW, 175) as yet another redemptive scheme, praising instead those artists (such as Paul Cézanne) who tried to depict a 'deanthropomorphized' nature, 'incommensurable with all human expressions whatsoever'.[124] This trend (in which he would later include Bram Van Velde) represented the 'one bright spot' in modern art: 'Even the portrait beginning to be dehumanized as the individual feels himself more & more hermetic & alone & his neighbour a coagulum as alien as a protoplast or God'.[125]

In Beckett's most relentlessly 'anti-anthropomorphic' text, *The Unnamable*, the voice treats the alluring idea of a human identity ('look, this is you, look at this photograph [...] to have no identity, it's a scandal' (SBT, 380)), or indeed a 'historical existence' (321), as a kind of siren song – or rather a hymn to the Lord – to be resisted at all costs: 'The instalment over, all joined in a hymn, Safe in the arms of Jesus, for example, or Jesus lover of my soul let me to thy bosom fly, for example' (321). Nefarious agents try to pressure the voice on this point, to no avail:

They also gave me the low-down on God. They told me I depended on him, in the last analysis. They had it on the reliable authority of their agents in Bally I forget what, this being the place, according to them, where the inestimable gift of life had been rammed down my gullet. But what they were most determined for me to swallow was my fellow-creatures.

> [...] They gave me courses on love, on intelligence, most precious, most precious. They also taught me to count, and even to reason. [...] Low types they must have been, their pockets full of poison and antidote. (300)

The poison–antidote dichotomy here invokes the issue of theodicy via its direct source in Samuel Johnson's *Idler* essay, number 89. The following passage was partly recorded by Beckett in one of the notebooks towards *Human Wishes*, his unfinished play about Johnson's life:[126]

> How evil came into the world; for what reason it is that life is overspread with such boundless varieties of misery; why the only thinking being of this globe is doomed to think merely to be wretched, and to pass his time from youth to age in fearing or in suffering calamities, is a question which philosophers have long asked, and which philosophy could never answer.
>
> Religion informs us that misery and sin were produced together. The depravation of human will was followed by a disorder of the harmony of nature; and by that *providence which often places antidotes in the neighbourhood of poisons*, vice was checked by misery, lest it should swell to universal and unlimited domination.[127]

For the unnameable voice, swallowing the notions of identity, historical existence, fellow creatures, love, reason and 'the inestimable gift of life' finally means swallowing the poison of dependence on God. This the voice will not do, for even if compliance might give access to a providential 'antidote', acceptance of the idea that all the 'misery' could ever be *worth it* through some greater good or restored harmony must be resisted absolutely. This text, then, ultimately fuses theodicy and 'anthropodicy' and pushes the rejection of both as far as is imaginable, on the axiomatic principle that existence as such, and not the depravation of human will, is to blame for 'original sin'.

Beckett and Dante

The impact of Dante on Beckett throughout his literary career is well documented, but Beckett's use of Dante as a staging ground for what I have called his *reductio ad Christianum* is less often noted. Beckett's appropriation of the term *gran rifiuto* cited before typifies this strategy. Dante's concern in this section of *Inferno* III is to expose the cowardice of those who refused to take any definite stand in life, thereby standing only for themselves: they remain unnamed, their precious reputation ('fama', line 49) obliterated, and their time-serving is symbolized in the banner chase. Beckett's student notes record the traditional identification of the 'refuser': 'Probably Celestino V, Pope in 1294, who abdicated after only 5 months in office. Dante purposely refers to him vaguely so that he may remain for ever in shameful obscurity.'[128] Beckett was well aware of Dante's system of moral allegory, and he takes the *gran rifiuto* as an emblem of his own approved aesthetics ('fidelity to failure') precisely because he sides with those who refuse to serve, and with the abject and rejected figures condemned by that system. Thus, Beckett challenges the legitimacy of the moral education that Dante the pilgrim undergoes (and that the poem pushes the reader to partake in), for instance through his repeated deployment of the 'superb pun'[129] on pity versus piety, 'Qui vive la pietà quand' è ben morta' (see *Inferno* XX, lines 28–30: 'Here pity lives when it is altogether dead. Who is more impious than he who sorrows at God's judgement?'). Beckett's most explicit counter-statement is in the poem 'Text' from 1931:

> We are proud in our pain
> our life was not blind.
> Worms breed in their red tears
> as they slouch by unnamed
> scorned by the black ferry
> despairing of death
> who shall not scour in swift joy
> the bright hill's girdle
> nor tremble with the dark pride of torture
> and the bitter dignity of an ingenious damnation.
>
> Lo-Ruhama Lo-Ruhama
> pity is quick with death.

(SBPo, 39)

As Daniela Caselli points out, most of the allusions here come from *Inferno* III:[130] in Dante, the life of these unnamed neutrals was precisely 'blind'; they have 'no hope of death' since they were 'never alive'; they are refused by both Heaven and deep Hell, thus they cannot enter Charon's ferry; their mingled blood and tears are gathered by worms as they fall. Beckett's note is defiance ('proud', *not* blind), and their double rejection becomes a badge of honour: by remaining outside both Heaven and Hell they become witnesses against an 'ingenious damnation', the forensic and frightening Dantean *contrapasso* which lays bare the nature of sins by their individual mode of punishment. 'Lo-Ruhama' invokes 'God's prophecy to Hosea that he will have no more mercy on the house of Israel' (Ackerley and Gontarski 2004: 559), an interjection that amplifies the poem's protest against the very idea of righteous judgement. Beckett's 'pity is quick with death' is not so much a translation of 'Qui vive la pietà ...' in this context, as a telling revision of Dante's meaning: 'piety' is here made to seem perverse and inappropriate, whereas the contemplation of residual life-in-death quickens pity. Years later, while designing his own infernal scenarios in *Happy Days* (1961), *Play* (1963) and *The Lost Ones* (1970), Beckett would invoke Dante indirectly through the phrase 'on the qui vive' (Ackerley and Gontarski 2004: 475). In each case, the point is to juxtapose a pitiless System, in which the characters are caught – Winnie's mound; the torturing spotlight forcing speech in *Play*; confinement to a cylinder and exitless tunnels in *The Lost Ones* – with the cruel need to nonetheless stay forever 'on the alert' (or undead) in such environments. To subscribe to 'piety' and the idea of righteous judgement in the face of such monstrosity is to place oneself on the side of the System; for the rhetoric of pity in Beckett's texts invariably supports the conclusion that metaphysical optimism equals wickedness.

Beckett, like Dante, thus seeks to interpellate and enlist the reader. A suitable emblem of this is his adoption of Dante's Belacqua (from *Purgatorio* IV) as indolent anti-hero. In a phrase admired by Beckett, Belacqua, from his curled-up embryonic posture, momentarily interrupts Dante and Virgil's ascent up the Mountain: 'Frate, l'andare in su che porta?' ('Oh brother, what is the use of going up?', line 127). The figure of Belacqua in Beckett's early fiction and beyond has been extensively discussed,[131] and in general it is clear that Beckett made him symbolic of withdrawal from the external universe into the 'wombtomb' (SBDr, 121) of the mind. The character of Murphy, tied to his rocking chair in order to come alive in his mind and experience the 'Belacqua bliss' (SBM, 111) represents the fullest development of this theme: in Beckett's words it is a 'surrender to the thongs of self, a simple materialization of self-bondage, acceptance of which is the fundamental unheroic. In the end it is better to perish than be freed'.[132] Once again, Beckett's approach to Dante is a combative one. There is no hint in Dante's treatment of this episode that Belacqua does not ultimately wish to ascend: he accepts the term of his confinement to Ante-Purgatory for his late repentance, but also hopes for prayers to speed him through the gate so that he can begin his purgation proper. For Beckett, though, he becomes a spanner in the works of the System: it is better to perish than be freed.

However, Beckett did not merely side with the outcasts of Dante's *Commedia*; he even suggested that Dantean damnation itself is too ordered and tame: 'I was, I was, they say in Purgatory, in Hell too, admirable singulars, admirable assurance. Plunged in ice up to the nostrils, the eyelids caked with frozen tears, to fight all your battles o'er again, what tranquility' (SBCP, 124–5). Despite this harsh punishment (drawn from *Inferno* XXXIII), its very terms imply a relatively stable identity in the punished subject: there is no question of which battles (or memories) belong to whom, or about the ability of each sufferer to believe and affirm that 'I was'. Beckett's most Dantesque fictional world in *How It Is* (1961) is also an attempt to go beyond Dante by issuing a sustained challenge to such 'tranquility'.

What, though, could be worse than the state in which the figures in *Inferno* VII, 109–26 (Beckett's main source here) find themselves? Above the surface of the river Styx, the Angry are drenched in mud and slime while forever tearing each other piecemeal with their teeth. Underneath the surface, unseen except for rising bubbles and unheard except for their low gurgles, are those who 'had been sullen in the sweet air that's gladdened by the sun / we bore the mist of sluggishness in us / now we are bitter in the blackened mud' (*Inferno* VII, lines 121–4). Beckett makes this mud the very element of *How It Is*: 'the tongue comes out lolls in the mud and no question of thirst either no question of dying of thirst either all this time vast stretch of time' (SBHI, 9). Here, too, snatches of the 'life above in the light' (8) are murmured forth by a voice, 'ill-said ill-heard ill-recaptured ill-murmured' (7). In Beckett's text the voice also shifts disorientatingly from without to within, 'on all sides then in me when the panting stops' (7). And when other figures are encountered in the mud, they too tear each other's flesh: in Beckett comically, with tin openers inserted into arse cheeks or used to inscribe the flesh with Roman capitals.

However, while Beckett adopts Dante's imagery of mud, he produces his own version of the System in which its creatures are immersed. Again, one indispensable context is Schopenhauer, as Shane Weller has pointed out (Weller 2009a: 39): in any conflict within the phenomenal world, the Will 'fails to recognize itself; seeking enhanced well-being in *one* of its phenomena, it produces great suffering in *another*', and thereby 'buries its teeth in its own flesh, not knowing that it injures always only itself [...] Tormentor and tormented are one' (Schopenhauer 1969: 354). The Many, seemingly separate and at odds, are in the end projections of the One: 'a million then if a million strong a million Pims now motionless agglutinated two by two in the interests of torment' (SBHI, 125). This vast procession or system of interchangeable beings ('Pim'/'Bam'/'Bom'/'Krim'/'Kram') is finally reduced back again: 'no never any Pim no nor any Bom no never anyone no only me' (159). Beckett is drawing here on his idiosyncratic appropriation of the Leibnizian monad.[133] Each monad for Leibniz is an extensionless unit of force or motion ('appetition'), which ultimately contains *all* representations within itself, some consciously 'apperceived' but the rest below the threshold as *petites perceptions*. Each monad is therefore a cosmos, but it is also hermetically isolated from all others, or 'windowless'; thus, the appearance of contact between a Pim and a Bom, say, is illusory, although both units are coordinated in their perceptions in a 'pre-established harmony' by the central monad, called God. In terms of the muddy world of *How It Is*, this means that each unit is ceaselessly driven onward by 'appetition'; receives a welter of confusing impressions that buzz momentarily into apperceptive focus from a voice that comes from both inside and outside the cosmos-containing self; and cannot ultimately distinguish itself either from this mass of representations or from the myriad other units with which it is somehow connected in pre-established 'harmony' ('we are regulated thus our justice wills it [...] it's mathematical it's our justice in this muck where all is identical' (SBHI, 121)). This world, then, produces no 'tranquility' whatever, and the physical tortures appear more and more as desperate attempts to elicit some reaction (a scream) from another being simply as proof, however scant, of both his identity and the narrator's own independent existence: 'only me no answer only me yes so that was true yes it was true about me yes and what's my name no answer WHAT'S MY NAME screams good' (159).

This will seem an odd point in the argument to invoke Dantean *amor* and Paradise, but in fact Beckett's text does so repeatedly (SBHI, 82):

> samples whatever comes remembered imagined no knowing life above life here God in heaven yes or no if he loved me a little if Pim loved me a little yes or no if I loved him a little in the dark the mud in spite of all a little

affection find someone at last someone find you at last live together glued
together.

As Shane Weller (2009a: 37) notes, the phrase 'glued together' recalls
the 'lethal glue' of love that binds Macmann and Moll in *Malone Dies*
and is 'frequently met with in mystic texts' (SBT, 264). It is worth
emphasizing how very different Beckett's attitude here is from other
appropriations of the Dantean blend of transcendent and carnal love
by his Modernist contemporaries. He is furthest, of course, from
T. S. Eliot, who finds in Dante an antidote to modern disorder, a lucid
awareness of 'every shade of both human and divine love. Beatrice is
his means of transition between the two, and there is never any danger of confounding the two loves'.[134] In *Paradiso* XXXI, Beatrice leads
Dante to the vision of the burning white rose of the tenth heaven,
pulsating with the saved. In Eliot's 'The Hollow Men' (1925) that 'mul-
tifoliate rose' is invoked without hope, whereas in 'Little Gidding'
(1942), after long purgation, a vision is granted of the 'crowned knot
of fire / And the fire and the rose are one': Eliot struggles towards con-
formity with the Dantean pattern (Mangianello 1980: 69–70). At the
other extreme there is Molly Bloom's joyous and insistently anti-
mystical (mock-Marian) carnality at the end of Joyce's *Ulysses*; having
wondered whether to wear a 'white rose' to seduce her husband-to-
be, she rejects this for 'a red one yes and how he kissed me under the
Moorish wall and I thought well as well him as another' (quoted in
Reynolds 1981: 80).[135] Both these models nonetheless approve of love
as such, but the glue that binds the 'lovers' in *How It Is* is, as Weller
points out, the cruelty of desire itself, grounded in Beckett's reading
of the Marquis de Sade's *120 Days of Sodom*. Beckett admired de Sade's
'dispassionate statement of 600 "passions"': 'The obscenity of surface
is indescribable. Nothing could be less pornographical. It fills me with
a sort of metaphysical ecstasy. The composition is extraordinary, as
rigorous as Dante's."[136] Cruelty in *How It Is*, too, is 'dispassionately'
stated, as in the 'table of basic stimuli one sing nails in armpit two
speak blade in arse' and so on (SBHI, 76), used to enforce reactions
from the other, including that of 'love': 'DO YOU LOVE ME CUNT'
(105). The rigour of Beckett's composition here, though, also involves
a very radical challenge to the Dantean paradigm of ascent towards
divine 'amor'. Let us recall Beckett's source for the 'love-glue' image in
Augustine's *Confessions*, chapter X: 'Out of all these things let my soul
praise Thee, O God, Creator of all; yet let not my soul be riveted unto

these things with the glue of love, through the senses of the body'
(SBDN, 14; see Weller 2009a: 37). Augustine's prayer is that he will
not be overly attached (glued) to the senses and thus free to praise
God; Beckett precisely reverses this by implying that mystic love and
the desire for God in heaven is *just another version* of cruel, Sadean love-
glue. As we shall now see, this is part of a critique not just of Dante,
but also of the approach to mysticism within Modernist writing more
generally.

The 'Need to Seem to Glimpse': Beckett and Mysticism

'Mysticism' understood as an intuitive, ahistorical, non-creedal contemplation of divine essence – a universal religious experience 'hardly
altered', in William James's words, 'by differences of clime or creed'
(quoted in Schmidt 2003: 287) – is in fact, as we saw in Chapter 1, a distinct and influential nineteenth-century construction. To recall Leigh
Eric Schmidt's analysis, the attractions of this concept were many:
it offered a way of safeguarding the validity of some version of religious experience versus both 'untrammelled naturalism' as well as
the excesses of outright occultism; it represented a definite departure
from the older tradition of Christian 'mystical theology' (ascesis, con-
templative prayer) or anagogical biblical exegesis; and it avoided association with religious 'enthusiasm', which in mid-eighteenth-century
critiques spelled sectarianism (Quakers, Methodists) and woman-
ish 'fanatic ecstasies and amorous extravagancies' (227). For James,
by contrast, ascetic visionaries should be 'manly', heroic, vital and
public-spirited (292). But the new concept of mysticism would also
prove flexible enough to be adapted by a secular feminist aesthete
like Virginia Woolf, who felt that 'behind the cotton wool is hidden a pattern; that we – I mean all human beings – are connected
with this; that the whole world is a work of art; that we are parts
of the work of art', yet 'certainly and emphatically there is no God;
we are the words; we are the music; we are the thing itself' (Woolf
2002: 85).

We have already gauged Beckett's reaction to this brand of uni-
versalized and aestheticized mysticism in his comment on Proust's
deployment of involuntary memory as just one more attempt to be 'a
good and faithful servant'. That is, Beckett recognizes this abstracted

'religious experience'[137] precisely as a neutered reformulation of Christian themes. One of his persistent reactions is satire, evident in his notes (for incorporation into the 1932 novel *Dream of Fair to Middling Women*) on William Inge's Bampton lectures, *Christian Mysticism* (1899). Thus for instance Beckett records the quaint description by Dionysius the Areopagite of God the Father as Neo-Platonic Monad, the 'hiddenness of the all transcending superessentially superexisting super-Deity' (SBDr, 17; SBDN, 99); or he playfully evokes a 'creedless, colourless, sexless Christ' in response to Inge's quotation of the idea of being symbolically 'transelemented' into Christ in the Eucharist (SBDr, 35; SBDN, 101). Even sharper is his scatological reaction to St John of the Cross' Dark Night as 'The Dark Shite of the Hole and the Ueberstench' (SBDN, 101), or his image of Julian of Norwich's famous 'All shall be well and all manner of thing shall be well' as a kind of menstrual flow, 'Eschatological catamenia' (102). The implicit point in all of these is that, however far the attempt to divest the deity of specific, earthly attributes is pushed, the overall project of salvation remains: in fact, that drive may be no less of a fundamental need than bodily excretion.

However, need and desire in Beckett is cruel. Thus Belacqua may attempt to withdraw to the 'wombtomb' (SBDr, 121) of the mind; or Murphy may try to approach the bliss of ultimate 'will-lessness, a mote in its absolute freedom' (SBM, 113); yet both remain 'dud mystics' (SBDr, 186),[138] suspended still between womb and tomb, and unable to will themselves into the will-less state. Watt tries another strategy, namely apprenticeship with a Master, Mr Knott, that knotty non-entity at one point described (as Chris Ackerley points out) in terms drawn from Dante's *Paradiso* X, his servants 'in tireless assuidity turning' about him (SBW, 52; Ackerley 2005: 84). Although Watt is dismissed without having gained access to the hiddenness of the all-transcending super-Deity, he still clings to the sense of having somehow drawn nearer: 'What had he learnt? Nothing. [...] But was not that something?' (SBW, 127). Of course, *Waiting for Godot* reworks the theme of attendance upon the absent Master in dramatic form. If he comes, they may perhaps be 'saved' yet waiting is a slow crucifixion. It matters little if Godot is or is not God, for there can in any case be no communication with 'divine apathia divine athambia divine aphasia' (SBCD, 42). Hope itself is cruel, and both *Watt* and *Godot* may be read as an assault upon that theological virtue along the lines set out in Beckett's 'Clare Street Notebook' in 1936:

There are moments where the veil of hope is finally ripped away and the eyes, suddenly liberated, see their world as it is, as it must be. Alas, it does not last long, the perception quickly passes: the eyes can only bear such a merciless light for a short while, the thin skin of hope re-forms and one returns to the world of phenomena. [...] And even if the cataract can be pierced for a moment it almost always re-forms immediately; and thus it is with hope.[139]

At this point, though, it becomes clear that Beckett's involvement with mysticism goes beyond satire, for the persistent 'need to seem to glimpse' (from 'what is the word', SBPo, 229) a realm somehow *beyond* the 'veil of hope' and the world of 'phenomena' is a theme repeatedly orchestrated in his own work.

The 'veil of hope' image here is derived from Schopenhauer:

At times, in the hard experience of our own sufferings or in the vividly recognized suffering of others, knowledge of the vanity and bitterness of life comes close to us who are still enveloped in the veil of Maya. We would like to deprive desires of their sting, close the entry to all suffering, purify and sanctify ourselves by complete and final resignation. But the illusion of the phenomenon soon ensnares us again, and its motives set the will in motion once more; we cannot tear ourselves free. The allurements of hope [...] rivet the bonds anew.

(Schopenhauer 1969: 379–80)[140]

The Hindu 'veil of Maya' is the realm of phenomenal illusion, and Schopenhauer draws on the Eastern mystical tradition in stating the aim of his philosophy, for 'what remains after the complete abolition of the will is, for all those who are still full of will, assuredly nothing. But also conversely, to those in whom the will has turned and denied itself, this very real world of ours, with all its suns and galaxies, is – nothing' (411–12). In a famous document, the letter to Axel Kaun from 1937, Beckett envisages language itself as a 'veil', which should be forcibly torn to allow the 'something or nothing' lurking behind it to seep through, in a 'whispering of the end-music or of the silence underlying all' (SBL1, 518–19). Beckett resists modern reformulations of Christian hope that appeal to a supposedly universal 'mystical' religious experience, but, in his own work, is the very hope of a Nothingness 'beyond hope' not itself liable to collapse into yet another mysticism of the *via negativa*? Are those 'liberated eyes' still in some way enacting the desire to see 'face to face' (1 Cor. 13:12)?[141]

Beckett was certainly aware of this possibility, for, as mentioned earlier, in two late interviews with Charles Juliet he distanced himself from both Schopenhauer and Eastern mysticism on the grounds that they still seek a residually religious 'solution', a 'way out' (Juliet 2009: 16, 39). Similarly, Beckett polices the 'fidelity to failure' even of a favourite artist like Bram Van Velde: he *must* have 'nothing to express, nothing with which to express, nothing from which to express, no power to express, no desire to express' (SBDi, 139), otherwise he might as well be painting a conventional Pietà or reposing in the bosom of St Luke. There is, however, no resolution in Beckett's own work to this dilemma of being always too close for comfort to Christianity. Instead, the tension itself is perpetually staged *within* his writing: 'Unnullable least. Say that best worse. With leastening words say least best worse. For want of worser worst. Unlessenable least best worse' (Beckett 2009a: 95).

Revising the Rhetoric of Apocalypse

To reiterate, Christianity remains Beckett's fundamental antagonist: and whereas a major trend of Modernist writing is to appropriate elements of Christian eschatology into some new religious, philosophical or aesthetic framework, Beckett deliberately reverses the trend by reducing these moves back to a more basic, underlying confrontation with Christianity itself. This approach is nowhere more evident than when dealing directly with the theme of a this-worldly Apocalypse within Modernism.

As we saw in Chapter 1, Roger Griffin has documented just how pervasive was the idea of apocalyptic 'renewal' within Modernist culture: the recipes were innumerable, but a fundamental pattern was 'decadence and regeneration', often involving a revolt against an oppressive sense of meaninglessness or *anomie* in order to overcome it and realize a vision of an entirely New Man.[142] It is revealing here to use Martin Heidegger's work as a contrast to Beckett's: partly because of his embrace of the Nazi version of apocalyptic nationalism, partly because of the derivation of his whole philosophy from an appropriation of Christian eschatology, but also because his association with Beckett's work has been persistent but is in fact entirely superficial.

Heideggerian 'authenticity' entails a heroic confrontation with one's own death, and with Nothingness. In his 1929 lecture 'What is Metaphysics?', this experience is paradoxically described as 'the bright night of the Nothing of Angst', through which the human being (*Dasein*) is able fully to recognize itself as 'not nothing': 'Only in the Nothing of Dasein does that-which-is come to itself according to its ownmost possibility.'[143] In *Endgame*, by contrast, Beckett parodies the whole attempt to wrest meaning from the Void:

> HAMM: We're not beginning to . . . to . . . mean something?
> CLOV: Mean something! You and I, mean something? (Brief laugh.) Ah that's a good one!
>
> (SBCD, 108)

But what if some 'rational being' should come back to earth and observe their play, might he not get 'ideas into his head' (108)?

> HAMM: [*Vehemently*] To think perhaps it won't all have been for nothing! (108)

Soon, Clov is pumping flea powder into his trousers to kill the last flea, for 'humanity might start from there all over again!' Reversing the cliché, Hamm's *fear* is precisely to remain not-nothing, living and residually significant.

Even without the context of Heidegger's conversion to Nazism, then, it should be evident that the heroic-redemptive attitude permeating all the philosopher's writings would constitute something like a paradigm case of 'recuperated failure' for the uncompromising Beckett. Accessing this context, though, reveals the political implications of Beckett's anti-redemptive stance. During his six-month German trip in 1936–37, Beckett sought out artists and dissidents who were persecuted by the regime, seeking especially to view officially scorned 'degenerate' art in private collections, museum cellars and even propaganda exhibitions. One of these banned artists, Karl Ballmer, interested Beckett intensely, and he studied the painter's pamphlet *Aber Herr Heidegger* (1933); a response to the infamous Freiburg Rectoral Speech (1933), wherein the party member Heidegger had affirmed his commitment to the 'spiritual mission that forces the destiny of the German people', and to the German academic community as purified *Kampfgemeinschaft* organized by the *Führerprinzip*. It is not known whether Beckett ever read the speech itself or indeed any Heidegger text.[144] His diary here concerns itself only with Ballmer and his art. He does, however, repeatedly record his feelings about the 'NS gospel': 'I say the expressions "historical necessity" and "Germanic destiny" start the vomit moving upwards.'[145] Nor is this attitude limited to just the Nazi regime; Beckett pounces whenever he detects any whiff of the kind of German Romanticism that is aligned with a New Dawn for the German People, the whole strain of apocalyptic nationalism of *Geist* that runs from the Napoleonic wars right through to the First World War.[146] For instance, during his visit to the Hamburger Kunsthalle, the Nazi attendant tried to 'convert' Beckett before two 'mornings' by Philip Otto Runge (1777–1810), strongly reminiscent of the 'dawn' imagery purveyed by much official Nazi art, 'but they make me feel ill'.[147] But even before his trip, writing on one of Heidegger's favourite poets[148] Rainer Maria Rilke in 1934, Beckett uses language that might conceivably have got him arrested in Germany. He accuses Rilke of trying always to 'rehabilitate the *Ichgott*', that 'prime article of the Rilkean faith, which provides for the interchangeability of Rilke and God'. Rilke has 'the fidgets': 'But why call the fidgets God, Ego, Orpheus and the rest? This is a childishness to which German writers seem specially prone' (SBDi, 67).

To conclude this section, a glance at important recent scholarship on the development of Heidegger's engagement with Christian eschatology will help us to draw a deeper contrast between Heidegger's and Beckett's respective *agons* with Christianity. In her recent book, Judith Wolfe convincingly refutes the idea that religion for Heidegger was ever a secondary concern; indeed, he 'discovered the phenomenological method, together with Protestantism, in large part as a means to adequately describing religious experience' (Wolfe 2013: 44). Wolfe documents in detail how Heidegger wrests his characteristic themes from a reworked Christian eschatology. 'Suffering', 'affliction' and the lack of 'security', for instance, are associated by him with the Pauline injunction to keep awake and sober for Christ's coming (1 Thess. 5). This suffering, however, is for Heidegger no longer focused on 'participation in Christ's passion' or 'a prolegomena to an experience of the divine', but is supposed to be 'in itself significant' (Wolfe 2013: 60). This is, Wolfe notes, an eschaton-less eschatology, for Christ's *parousia*, the traditional object of hope itself, is missing, even while Heidegger attempts to endow the affliction (*Bedrängnis*) of waiting itself with independent significance: 'Consequently, *Angst* (anxiety, affliction) and not hope is the dominant mood of eschatological expectation and the mood most revelatory of Dasein's own being' (83). Precisely in order to redeem eschatological expectation, therefore, Heidegger advocates an 'ontological' waiting upon Being-as-such over the 'ontic science' of theology.

Beckett, by contrast, does not wish to redeem eschatological expectation but to assault it. Clov's opening words in *Endgame* go to the heart of this distinction: 'Finished, it's finished, nearly finished, it must be nearly finished. [*Pause.*] Grain upon grain, one by one, and one day, suddenly, there's a heap, a little heap, the impossible heap' (SBCD, 93). Christ's *consummatum est* from the Cross is revoked by the simple word 'nearly', and by the Zeno-like[149] grains-that-never-make-a-heap, suggesting, in Beckett's words to Alan Schneider, 'the impossibility of catastrophe. Ended at its inception, and at every subsequent instant, it continues, ergo can never end'.[150] The rules of Beckett's game are always the same: evoke the desire for an end (always shadowed by the Christian End), and then disappoint it cruelly. 'Let us pray to God' / 'The bastard! He doesn't exist!' (SBCD, 119). Where Heidegger might think he can in fact overcome Christianity, Beckett has no such illusions: 'Use your head can't you, use your head, you're on earth, there's no cure for that! [*Pause.*] Get out of here and love one another! Lick your neighbour as yourself!' (125). There ain't no cure for love: for Beckett this is the grimmest of conclusions, but it is also the engine that drives his work and keeps the endgame going, since disappointment and frustration could not finally be imagined without it.

The Conclusion, in Which Nothing Is Concluded

> Of those wishes that they had formed they well knew that none could be obtained. They deliberated awhile what was to be done, and resolved, when the inundation should cease, to return to Abissinia.
>
> – Samuel Johnson, *Rasselas* (Johnson 2009: 109)

It is not surprising that *Rasselas* should be one of Beckett's favourite books by Johnson. The tale of the pampered Prince of Abissinia who elopes with his friends from the soporific 'happy valley' of his birth to seek happiness through adventure but, having realized that earthly desire is unobtainable, merely returns to the starting point, is an allegory which would have appealed to Beckett's sense of circularity and 'the vanity of human wishes'. Beckett in fact worked on and off for four years (1937–40) on a prospective play on Johnson's life to be entitled *Human Wishes* after Johnson's poem: a short fragment and three thick preparatory notebooks are all that remain of this project. What drew Beckett to Johnson was the older Sam's fierce combination of existential despair and Christianity, the one element perpetually heightening the other:

> It isn't Boswell's wit and wisdom machine that means anything to me, but the miseries that he never talked of, being unwilling or unable to do so. The horror of annihilation, the horror of madness, the horrified love of Mrs Thrale, the whole mental monster ridden swamp that after hours of silence could only give some ghastly bubble like 'Lord have mercy upon us'. The background of the *Prayers and Meditations*. The opium eating, dreading-to-go to bed, praying-for-the-dead, past living, terrified of dying, terrified of deadness, panting on to 75 bag of water, with a hydracele on his right testis. How jolly.[151]

The 'ghastly bubble' is a sudden ejaculatory prayer, which, as it were, pushes itself to the surface. In his notebooks, Beckett consecutively recorded two examples of this spiritual eruption from the *Prayers and Meditations*:

> Since my resolution formed last Easter I have made no advancement in knowledge or in goodness; nor do I recollect that I have endeavoured it. I am dejected but not hopeless.
>   O God for Jesus Christ's sake have mercy upon me.
>   (Sept. 1764)
>
> Since the last Easter I have reformed no evil habits, my time has been improfitably spent & seems as a dream that has left nothing behind. My memory grows confused & I know not how the days pass over me.
>   Good Lord deliver me (Easter 1765)[152]

Beckett's fascination with these 'bubbles' emerging out of silence and inner darkness points to a less-known aspect of his aesthetic thought, and adds another twist to the account given in this chapter. In his 'German diary' (15 November 1936), Beckett spoke of 'art as prayer': 'the art (picture) that is a prayer sets up prayer, releases prayer in onlooker, i.e. Priest: Lord have mercy upon us. People: Christ have mercy upon us' (quoted in Knowlson 1997: 237). It would seem as though a perpetual dialectic between a last-ditch, desperate prayer for Christ's mercy (the 'ghastly bubble') and its disappointment is at the heart of Beckett's 'anti-redemptive' aesthetic. Of course, this does not mean that Christianity is prominent on the surface of every Beckett text. Nonetheless, his relentless assault on redemptive schemes that in the end amount only to watered-down Christianity, and his self-imposed unending ethical task of 'fidelity to failure', continually evoke this fundamental dialectic. But in literary terms, this also means that the prayer itself must be stated as fully as its deflation, and so even a text as radically cruel as *How It Is* can contain surprises:

> a moment of the tender years the lamb black with the world's sins the world cleansed the three persons yes I assure you and that belief the feeling since then ten eleven that belief said to have been mine the feeling since then vast stretch of time that I'd find it again the blue cloak the pigeon the miracles he understood

> (SPHI, 77)

In examining 'Modernism and Christianity' through the lens of Beckett's texts, and tracing his rejection of the very notion of conclusively 'overcoming' Christianity, the critic too may be said to embark on a return to the starting point: the keen recovery of those live, formative, unpredictable tensions that remain intrinsic to this field of study.

CONCLUSION: MODERNISM AND CHRISTIANITY AS A FIELD OF STUDY

This book has made use of a range of incisive studies of single authors, specific issues or movements, and theoretical themes that are relevant to 'Modernism and Christianity', but as I noted at the outset, no previous attempt has been made to systematically outline a distinct field of Modernism and Christianity studies. It is no exaggeration to say that the conjunction is not in fashion: among the 56 chapters of the recent *Oxford Handbook of Modernisms* (2010), just one discusses Christianity, and that very briefly, within the limiting context of 'Religion, Psychical Research, Spiritualism'.[153] If the reader has got this far in the present book, such neglect should seem not just quaint but shocking, and in need of some explanation.

Leon Surette has already outlined the beginnings of such an explanation in *The Birth of Modernism*: 'Although scepticism and relativism are undoubtedly the two definitional dogmas of modern enlightened academic humanism, it is far from obvious that they are the guiding principles of modernism' (1993: 161). This conflation can skew critical and historical perceptions and lead to an almost casual neglect of the impact of Christianity upon Modernism. For instance, Surette points out that 'it is playing rather fast and loose with the term [scepticism] to count Walter Pater and William James as sceptics because of their rejection of Christianity [. . .] and it is thoroughly misleading to describe the credulous W. B. Yeats as a sceptic' (164). While many Modernists may have been 'sceptical with respect to Christianity', it is also the case that many of them were 'credulous with respect to spiritual, visionary, or mystical doctrines and beliefs' (164), and, one might add, political religions such as revolutionary Marxism and Fascism. It will not do, then, to make a critically approved 'negative attitude to Christianity' into a 'touchstone for scepticism' (164), for this conceals the extremely diverse attitudes that in fact assembled under the banner of anti-Christianity: and as we have seen in this book, such a rallying against Christianity is an important part of the historical development of the very term 'Modernism' itself. Instead, the effort to recover historically the formative tensions between Modernism and Christianity enables us to see how *different* the assumptions and influences of past thinkers and cultural or political actors may be from our own. Christianity was, at the birth of Modernism, a force to be seriously reckoned with by all: again, the very idea of a New Era or epoch could not be defined except through a specific imaginative construction of the Old. Central to Modernism and Christianity studies, then, should be the critical deployment of Christianity as a unique barometer of Modernist worldviews and aesthetic projects, since a taxonomy of their creative constructions of Christianity's past, present and future can function as a crucial tool in charting and comparing Modernisms.

It has been a fundamental assumption of this study that dense contextualization, biographical information and archival study are essential to this effort of historical recovery if we are to come to grips with the sheer evolving complexity of specific 'formative tensions' at work in Modernism. Furthermore, interdisciplinary work is needed far beyond the present contribution: insights from intellectual, cultural, political and scientific history, and from theology, philosophy, psychology, anthropology and sociology can all contribute to outlining the backdrop to such tensions, which after all concern nothing less than the course of Western modernity itself. Interdisciplinary work on Modernism and Christianity *across the arts* (and thus of course well beyond the confines of Anglophone writing) is also clearly needed. Alongside the need for empirically oriented historical recovery runs a need for further theoretical reflection: what concepts are best suited for capturing the richness, complexity and ambiguity of the many relationships between Modernism and Christianity? Furthermore, how should the recovery of this formative relationship affect our sense of the subsequent historical development of 'post'-Modernism? And finally, how may the critic's own philosophical and methodological commitments be colouring his or her approach to this field?

The case studies in this book have attempted to merge theoretical reflection and individual creative complexity, examining and measuring such ideas as Catholic Modernisms, dogma and the crisis of authority, theodicy, Dantean influence, mysticism and apocalypticism against the thought and *oeuvres* of those 'highly sensitive conducting-rods', James Joyce, David Jones, T. S. Eliot, Ezra Pound, W. H. Auden and Samuel Beckett. In doing so, it has become clear that the possible attitudes of Modernists to Christianity are varied and nuanced; and whether the stress is on 'struggle and rejection', 'conversion', 'return', 'appropriation' or the 'impossibility of overcoming', the analysis has tended to lead us towards the heart of the aesthetic and cultural projects of these writers generally. Hopefully, then, these readings offer a limited demonstration of the fruitfulness of the approach to the field of Modernism and Christianity outlined in this study. Hopefully, too, the reader will realize just how much work remains to be done, so that the present conclusion may indeed be one 'in which nothing is concluded'.

NOTES

1. In question here is *not* the 'modernist crisis' within Catholic theology, discussed in Chapter 2.
2. This formulation is indebted to Perl 1984: 12, discussed below.
3. A classic account here is Berman 1982.
4. Griffin cites Bauman 1991 and Koselleck 1988 here.
5. For further discussion of these terms, see pp. 15–20. For an excellent overview of the complex permutations of the idea of 'nihilism' within Modernism, see Weller 2011.
6. Griffin here draws on Frank Kermode, *The Sense of Ending* (Kermode 2000). The forthcoming conference volume *Modernism, Christianity, and Apocalypse* (ed. Erik Tonning, Matthew Feldman and David Addyman, Brill, 2013) represents an attempt to build on Kermode's and Griffin's insights in this field. (A selection of talks from the conference are available online at www.backdoorbroadcasting. net). See also the comments on Heidegger and Beckett in Chapter 4 of this book.
7. In this book, generic fascism is non-capitalized, whereas reference to the Fascism of Mussolini's (or Hitler's) regimes is signalled by capitalization.
8. Griffin adopts this term from Berger 1967.
9. Letter to Vanessa Bell, 11 February 1928, in Woolf 1975–80: III, 457–8.
10. On Woolf's brand of secular mysticism, see Chapter 4, p. 115. Woolf's 'moments of being', often set against a threatening darkness and chaos, perfectly illustrate Griffin's concept of 'epiphanic' Modernism; though to label all artistic Modernism in this way is of course bound to be no more than a heuristic gesture.
11. See n. 29.
12. See n. 49.
13. Of course this is far from exhausting the possibilities; in fact a subsection of the current book series called 'Modernism, Christianity and . . .' could easily be imagined, with such third terms as 'Marxism', 'Fascism', 'Feminism', 'Eugenics', 'Darwinism', 'Anthropology', 'Myth', 'Psychoanalysis', 'Nihilism' and so on. (For a suggested approach to nihilism, see the next section.) The particular 'formative tensions' discussed in this section have been selected to illustrate the themes of 'revitalization', epochal transformation and the general religious impulse in Modernism that are central to this argument.
14. Of course, 'revitalization' is, as we have seen, a more general Modernist concern; T. S. Eliot or W. H. Auden are not 'vitalists', for instance; Marxists were generally not vitalists and so on. Furthermore, to hold a vitalist philosophy does not make one a Modernist, unless it is combined with formal or cultural experimentalism of some kind.
15. All translations from Vassenden's original Norwegian are my own.

16. See Ottomeyer 2013. For the fullest treatment of Haeckel's life and ideology, including an account of his relationship to Christianity, see Richards 2008.
17. My treatment of Nietzsche and Bergson here summarizes that of Vassenden 2012, ch. 2.
18. For more on Nietzsche and *ressentiment*, see the next section.
19. For a detailed reading of this text and its manuscript versions, see T. R. Wright's excellent *D. H. Lawrence and the Bible*, ch. 13 (Wright 2000).
20. However, see Purdy 1994 and Armstrong 2013 (ch. 6) for some incisive starting points.
21. This heading alludes to the title of Michael Allen Gillespie, *The Theological Origins of Modernity* (Gillespie 2009), which develops an independent but overlapping argument to those pursued by Milbank and Taylor (described below). While I do not have space to discuss Gillespie's account here, this book is hereby recommended to the reader as a useful supplement to theirs.
22. Lewis's analysis of individual authors and his attempt to link social theory, religion and Modernist novels make his book a major contribution in this field. Unfortunately I only have space here to state my methodological disagreement with him in the barest terms, which do no justice to his contribution.
23. For the best study of Beckett's anti-rationalist reading of Western metaphysics based around the pre-Socratics and Schopenhauer, see Feldman 2006. See also Tonning 2011.
24. See Milbank 2006, ch. 10 for a discussion of the 'ontology of violence/peace'.
25. See especially Milbank 2006, Cunningham 2002 and Pickstock 1998. These are complex and much-discussed studies, and the object of the present discussion is simply to map them onto 'Modernism and Christianity studies', which, I argue, cannot overlook them. For a helpful summary of Milbank's thesis in *Theology and Social Theory*, see Kerr 1992; for an anthology of central 'Radical Orthodoxy' texts with a useful introduction, see Milbank and Oliver (eds) 2009.
26. 'Indeed, we might, following John Milbank, see this new "univocal" understanding of being, predicated alike of God and of creatures, as the crucial shift from which other changes flow' (Taylor 2007: 774).
27. See Milbank 2006: 280–95 for a discussion of Nietzschean genealogy and *ressentiment*.
28. There is unfortunately no space in this chapter to discuss Jones's work in his main profession as painter, engraver and sculptor. For the most complete account, see Miles and Shiel 2003.
29. Letter to Nora Barnacle, 29 August 1904, quoted in Lernout 2010: 102–3.
30. Inge 1919: 1, quoted in Fordham forthcoming.
31. Pitcher 1907: 372, quoted in Fordham forthcoming.
32. See Leon Surette's perceptive comments in *The Birth of Modernism*: 'Nonetheless, at the time that [M]odernism was being born, Nietzscheanism, Marxism, positivism, and occultism all perceived Christianity as a common antagonist – just as occultism, Protestantism, and Jacobinism had all seen Rome as their common antagonist at the end of the eighteenth century. These shared antagonisms have often confused observers of the cultural history of [M]odernism – and not infrequently confused the players themselves' (Surette 1993: 94).
33. In Joyce's 'Pola notebook' (entry of 15 November 1904), he draws a similar lesson from Aquinas, from the point of view of perception rather than making: 'But

the activity of recognition is, like every other activity, itself pleasant and there-fore every object that has been apprehended is secondly in whatsoever measure beautiful. Consequently even the most hideous object may be said to be beauti-ful for this reason as it is *a priori* said to be beautiful in so far as it encounters the activity of simple perception' (Joyce 2008b: 106). My thanks to Finn Fordham for alerting me to this source.

34. Letter to Stanislaus Joyce, 13 November 1906, quoted in Lernout 2010: 106.

35. See n. 29.

36. S. Joyce 1962, quoted in Lernout 2010: 98.

37. Letter to Nora Barnacle, *c.*1 September 1904, quoted in Lernout 2010: 103.

38. Letter to Stanislaus Joyce, 3 December 1904, quoted in Lernout 2010: 103.

39. *Summa Theologica*, I–II, q. 57, a. 5, ad 1ᵐ, quoted in Noon 1957: 29.

40. For a short biography of Jones, see Aldritt 2003.

41. From Fry's Introduction to the *Catalogue of the Second Post-Impressionist Exhibition*, quoted in Spalding 1980: 160.

42. According to a letter to René Hague from February 1972 (CD1/15, Jones collection, National Library of Wales), Jones always encountered resistance from Catholic friends to the analogy between the work of the artist and the priest's action at Mass, and Hague himself felt that this analogy was taken to extremes by Jones. My thanks to Thomas Goldpaugh for sharing a draft for a forthcoming article which discusses this letter.

43. In 'Art and Sacrament' Jones comments that while he is convinced that 'man remains, by definition, man-the-artist', that conviction 'will furnish no lorica or padding against the dilemmas and quandaries. Indeed, it is that conviction which strips off all defensive armour, so that the sharp contradictions and heavy incon-gruities may at least be felt. Vulnerability is essential, or we may not notice the dichotomy even if it exists' (DJEA, 178).

44. Roger Griffin argues that revolutionary political programmes 're-imagining the future as a permanently "open" site for the realization of utopias within historical time' (Griffin 2007: 54) can fruitfully be considered as examples of Modernism in their own right. See ch. 6 of Griffin 2007 for a genealogy of political Modernism, 1848–1945.

45. This word, oft-repeated by Jones in essays and correspondence, derives from his reading of Oswald Spengler's *The Decline of the West* (see Staudt 1994: 118).

46. To Harman Grisewood, Jones wrote that 'I *like* the way Chamberlain treated Adolf as a truculent adolescent who needed to be understood' (4 October 1938; quoted in Dilworth 1986: 158).

47. See ch. 5 in Tom Villis's recent *British Catholics and Fascism* (Villis 2013) for a care-ful treatment of the attitudes of three of Jones's Catholic friends, Tom Burns, Bernard Wall and Christopher Dawson, in relation to fascism. Villis also discusses Jones's case in ch. 7, arguing that the poet 'believed that Hitler was *both* a rebuke to the decadence of the Western world and a horrific dicta-tor who unleashed a disastrous war. [. . .] Nazism was the imperfect and ter-rifying realisation of a necessary revolt' (179). Another complex example is J. H. Oldham's group 'The Moot', which began meeting in April 1938 (see Clements 2010: 37). Oldham issued a proposed manifesto for the group entitled 'A Reborn Christendom' in August 1939 (published in Oldham 1940), arguing that a reborn Christendom 'can only mean something which, if it were to come to

pass, the historian of the future would regard as having comparable historical significance with the new social doctrines and systems which have merged in our time' (Institute of Education, London, Moot Papers, no. 2). See Jonas Kurlberg's forthcoming article 'The Moot, the End of Civilisation, and the Re-birth of Christendom' (Kurlberg forthcoming).

48. For further details on this passage, see Mangianello 1980: 111–14, and Cheng 1995: 221–2.

49. Griffin acknowledges that Modernists, especially 'programmatic' or political ones, could also be 'entranced rather than exhausted by Modernity, and [...] feel spurred on to formulate projects for its transcendence within an alternative modernity the other side of decadence at the end of the tunnel' (Griffin 2007: 67). Furthermore, he interprets Marxism itself as a form of Modernism, stressing its 'attempt to re-erect a sacred canopy appropriate to the age of secularizing modernity, one based on the revolutionary ethic of social justice and human compassion' (174). Marxism can be assessed 'as a modern version of millenarianism, political religion, or Gnosticism' (174). Both Joyce's embrace of this or that feature of modernity and his socialist leanings could thus potentially be accounted for by Griffin's framework. Nevertheless, taking the Catholic Church as the fundamental antagonist of progress and positive change enables a construction of 'modernity', not as a threat or malaise, but as a broadly salutary development that is not-yet-complete (but requires the final overcoming of the Church and its 'reactionary' allies, and, in Joyce's case, the re-imagination of the ordinary as the sacred). There is a 'revolutionary' dynamic here: but Joyce's version does not in fact rely on a construction of *modernity*-as-decadence. On the contrary, Joyce lauds the 'vivisective' modern spirit: 'Vivisection itself is the most modern process one can conceive. The ancient spirit accepted phenomena with a bad grace. The ancient method investigated law with the lantern of justice, morality with the lantern of revelation, art with the lantern of tradition. But all these lanterns have magical properties: they transform and disfigure. The modern method examines its territory by the light of day. [...] All modern political and religious criticism dispenses with presumptive States, and presumptive Redeemers and Churches' (JJSH, 186).

50. See n. 34.

51. Letter to Harriet Shaw Weaver, 24 November 1926; Joyce 1966: 146.

52. In a youthful essay on 'Force' (1898), Joyce 'maintained that subjugation of men by force is futile, and expressed a hatred of violence which proved to be lifelong'; the artist's method, instead, is 'persuasion' (Mangianello 1980: 75). This is rooted in Joyce's attraction to anarchism.

53. Biblical quotations in this chapter are from the Douay-Rheims translation, whereas subsequent chapters cite the Authorized Version (see the bibliography for details).

54. Draft letter of February or March 1952, National Library of Wales catalogue number CF 2/17.

55. For details, see Lang 1993: chs 7–9.

56. This is debatable, since Christmas morning is the time for the soldiers' 'communion' mentioned earlier, and the night before, the German soldiers are heard singing 'Es ist ein' Ros' entsprungen' across No Man's Land. Yet the British soldiers respond with a coarse music-hall song ('Casey Jones'), which

significantly 'unmade his harmonies' (DJIP, 67–8). My point is simply that the poem does admit twinges of doubt, in line with the emphasis on 'vulnerability' quoted in n. 43.

57. See especially Dilworth 1988, Staudt 1994 and Robichaud 2007. The facts about Jones's reading of Joyce mentioned here are recorded in these studies.

58. National Library of Wales, David Jones Collection, catalogue number LE 1/36. My thanks to Anna Johnson for sharing her transcription of this handwritten manuscript draft, which probably dates from the late 1950s.

59. Emilio Gentile is the leading proponent of this term, especially within the modern historiography of interwar totalitarianism; but he also points out how contemporary observers themselves consistently characterized these movements as political religions. See Gentile 2000: 40–9.

60. This is meant to invoke Roger Griffin's decadence–renewal pattern as central to Modernism (see Griffin 2007, chs 2 and 3). As discussed in the first two chapters of this book, a 'revitalized' Christianity could be as effective and attractive as for instance occultism or fascism in this process for some thinkers.

61. See Schuchard (1999: 131–47) for a fine reading of Baudelaire's significance for Eliot.

62. Compare Eliot's well-known letter to Paul Elmer More on 20 February 1928, discussing 'the void that I find in the middle of all happiness and human relations', wherein 'only Christianity helps to reconcile me to life, which is otherwise disgusting' (quoted in Schuchard 1999: 152).

63. The 1894 trial against the Jewish officer Alfred Dreyfus became a rallying point for both pro- and anti-Semitic feeling in France in the 1890s. Since Anthony Julius's *T. S. Eliot, Anti-Semitism, and Literary Form* (1995), debate has raged over the real extent and influence of Eliot's own (demonstrable) prejudice against Jews. Two issues of *Modernism/modernity* (nos 1 and 3 in vol. 10, 2003) include arguments from several prominent scholars, and Spurr (2010) provides an appendix on the issue. While there is no space for detailed comment here, I would note that the early Eliot is more hostile to Jewishness than the later. See e.g. *The Idea of a Christian Society* (1939), which notes that Jesus was 'wholly Semitic on both sides' (Eliot 1976: 56). It was common among anti-Semites who wanted to enlist Christians to ignore or revise Christ's Jewishness, but Eliot resists this. The criticism he received after his infamous comment about 'free-thinking Jews' in *After Strange Gods* (1933), and his personal contact with exiled and persecuted German Jews such as Karl Mannheim and Adolf Löwe in the late 1930s and throughout the war, appears to have made him rethink or tone down his attitudes.

64. For a reading of *The Waste Land* along these lines, see Asher 1995: 42–4.

65. For 'creative destruction' in Modernism, see Griffin 2007: 54.

66. In his contributions to the think-tank *The Moot* (1938–47), Eliot would repeatedly apply this litmus test. For instance, commenting (1 January 1941) on J. H. Oldham's proposal for a 'Fraternity of the Spirit', Eliot argued that Oldham's vague, inclusive use of the word 'spirit' tended to ignore the Evil Spirit (MS 9/3/81, J. H. Oldham Papers [Moot Papers], New College Library, University of Edinburgh; thanks to Jonas Kurlberg for this reference); see also Eliot's comments on J. M. Murry's idea of a National Church, quoted below.

67. Asher argues that the shift to supernaturalism was Eliot's way of 'elevating his [political] preferences to the level of mythology' (1995: 63), in a partly

strategic move; but this to me understates Eliot's earnestness and intellectual commitment.

68. See Eliot's letter to Geoffrey Faber, 18 September 1927: 'There is another "good thing" of life too, which I have had only in flashes. It is the sudden realization of being separated from all enjoyment, from all things of this earth, even from Hope; a sudden separation and isolation from *everything*; and at that moment of illumination, a recognition of the fact that one can do without all these things, a joyful recognition of what John of the Cross means when he says the soul cannot be possessed of the divine union until it has divested itself of the craving for all created beings' (Eliot 2012: 712–13).

69. For this statement from the 25 April 1948 issue of the journal *Aspects de la France et du Monde*, see Asher 1995: 130–1.

70. The quotation is from a 1937 BBC broadcast reprinted by Eliot as an appendix to *Idea*.

71. MS 14/6/21, J. H. Oldham Papers (Moot Papers), New College Library, University of Edinburgh. Eliot's paper was written between the first (1–4 April 1938) and the second meeting (23–6 September 1938). My thanks to Jonas Kurlberg for this dating, and for drawing the source to my attention.

72. 'The Little Review Calendar', *The Little Review* (Spring 1922), reprinted in EPPer, II, 220. This was not the first time Pound had thus announced this 'end', however. The phrase first appeared in an advert he wrote for *BLAST*, on the back of *The Egoist*, 1 April 1914. My thanks to Henry Mead for this point.

73. This well-known quotation comes from 'Psychology and Troubadours' (quoted here in Surette 1993: 31).

74. On this topic, see Perl 1984, chs 1 and 8.

75. My thanks to Andrea Rinaldi for identifying this allusion.

76. The most detailed account of this topic is Surette 1999, which I rely on here for details.

77. A detailed account of Pound's admiration for Mussolini is given in Redman 1991, ch. 4, on which this account is based.

78. Letters to Oswald Mosley, 24 March 1938 ('I also believe my USURY canto cd/ be more fully used') and 31 March 1939 ('I come back to fact that ACTION has NOT YET printed my usury canto/ this is something that anyone else wd/ have to pay sold [sic] cash for'). YCAL MSS 43, box 36, folder 1495. My thanks to Matthew Feldman for sharing his transcriptions. See his forthcoming monograph *Ezra Pound's Fascist Propaganda 1935–1945* (Feldman 2013).

79. Radio speech, 1942, YCAL MSS 43, Box 129, Folder 5392. Thanks to Matthew Feldman for sharing his transcription.

80. Of course, this is in no way news to Pound scholars; see, for instance, Bush 1976: 289, arguing that 'Dante combined with Douglas in Pound's mind to make usury not just a contemporary problem but the *Cantos*' most important emblem of the fall of the "green world" of natural bounty', for usury in Pound 'perverts the bounty and sustenance of *God's* art, which is nature'.

81. Aquinas 2008: Secunda Secundae Partis, Q. 78, Art. 1.

82. 'Mr. Eliot's Looseness', *New English Weekly* (10 March 1934), in EPPer, VIII, 174.

83. 'Date Line' (1934), in Pound 1968: 85.

84. Pound, letter to Odon Por, May 1936, quoted in Surette 1993: 273. The book was *Il giusto prezzo mediovale* (1913) by Luigi Pasquale Cairoli.

85. Letter of March 1936, YCAL MSS 43, Box 37, folder 1536. Another letter in April (same folder) states that 'If you mean to be NEW, NEO etc. you can't relapse into a darkness that preceded either Aquinas or "Quadrigessimo Anno".' My thanks to Andrea Rinaldi for sharing these documents.

86. This was a favourite dismissive word in Pound's post-war correspondence with Olivia Rossetti Agresti (herself Catholic); see Pound 1998: 40, 43, 88, 139, 212.

87. Pound's tag in Canto LXXXVIII (EPCan, 291), translating Eriugena's 'Omnia quae sunt, lumina sunt'; see Brooke-Rose 1971: 116, for an account of the source.

88. See Canto XXXVI, EPCan, 179; for a discussion see Liebregts 2004: 220–1.

89. Pound, 'Statues of Gods', *The Townsman*, August 1939 (EPSP, 71).

90. Pound's draft for this article, dated 7 August 1939, is reprinted in Bacigalupo 2001; for the quoted passage see 230–1 (note that Pound 1996b omits it).

91. In one broadcast from 28 March 1942, Pound told his listeners that 'every sane act you commit is committed in homage to Mussolini and Hitler' (quoted in Feldman 2012: 89).

92. FBI interrogation of Pound, conducted 8 May 1945, War Office File; my thanks to Matthew Feldman for this information.

93. See Pound's article 'Il Grano', *Meridiano di Roma*, VI. 36 (7 September 1941), reprinted in EPPer, VIII, 138–40. See Rinaldi (forthcoming) for a preliminary study of this imagery.

94. See Sider 1980, on which I base my account of Tertullian.

95. Original and translation (by Pierre Bühler) quoted in Bühler 2008: 132, n. 4.

96. Letter to Olivia Rossetti Agresti, 2 September 1953 (Pound 1998:122).

97. See Mendelson 1999: 89–90 for details.

98. The following paragraph synthesizes Auden's views from a number of wartime essays, not always chronologically, in order to clarify connections between his ideas that often remain implicit in individual formulations. The chronology is retrievable in APr II. See also the Index for Auden's works.

99. Mendelson (1999: 150) remarks that Auden found the influence of the *Action Française* 'pernicious'.

100. Mendelson (1999: 190) briefly notes Auden's use of Charles Williams's term 'co-inherence' in the Simeon section of *For the Time Being*, but does not treat Williams's influence on Auden's understanding of Incarnation in this work in any detail. McAlonan (2006: 225) notes Ursula Niebuhr's comment pointing out Auden's idiosyncratic focus on Incarnation in her husband's book, but does not connect this with his reading of Williams.

101. Auden made this term his own, often without acknowledgement, e.g. 'the invisible co-inherence of souls' ('Lecture Notes', December 1942; APr II, 172).

102. In a 1956 introduction to Williams's *Descent*, Auden noted that the book was uniquely 'imbued with ecumenical passion' (APr IV, 29), and Auden's own sympathies are similarly eclectic. It is worth noting that Auden will filter the Protestant Niebuhr on Incarnation through the 'Catholic' idea of substitution.

103. See Kirsch (2005: 10–14) for an account of the importance of the idea of an *agape*-community in Auden's 1933 poem 'A Summer's Night'.

104. Auden, *New Year Letter*, ACP, 241.

105. McDiarmid (1990: 88–9) makes a similar point.

106. See Mendelson (1981: 225–6) for a discussion of the word 'crooked'.

107. Auden, letter to his father, 13 October 1942, quoted in Mendelson 1999: 186.

108. Auden, letter to Kallmann, Christmas Day 1941, quoted in Mendelson 1999: 182.

109. Auden probably developed a point from Niebuhr (1964: 184) here: 'The parent is anxious about his child and this anxiety reaches beyond the grave. Is the effort of the parent to provide for the future of the child creative or destructive? Obviously it is both. It is, on the one hand, an effort to achieve the perfection of love by transcending the limits of finiteness and anticipating the needs of the child beyond the death of the parent. On the other hand, as almost every last will and testament reveals, it betrays something more than the perfection of love. It reveals parental will-power reaching beyond the grave and seeking to defy death's annulment of parental authority.' This, then, is what Mary must atone for.

110. The Christian religion is unique because it 'believes that the Unconditional was objectively manifested upon one unique occasion (The Word was made Flesh and dwelt among us) and thenceforth is subjectively manifest, perpetually and to all' (APr II, 163).

111. This is the topic of Surette's *The Birth of Modernism*; see especially Surette 1993: ch. 2.

112. Pound, 'The State', in *The Exile*, Spring 1927, 1; quoted in Perl 1984: 261.

113. For connections between 'epiphanic' and 'programmatic' (sociopolitical) Modernism, see Griffin 2007: 61–4.

114. My thanks to Matthew Feldman for this point.

115. Nevertheless, as argued in Matthew Feldman's *Ezra Pound's Fascist Propaganda 1935–1945*, Pound was also a 'committed, informed and influential propagandist for fascist ideology' who remained close to the party line (Feldman 2013: ch. 1).

116. Further documentation on Beckett and Christianity may be found in Mary Bryden's excellent study *Samuel Beckett and the Idea of God* (Bryden 1998) and Iain Bailey's forthcoming *Samuel Beckett and the Bible* (Bailey forthcoming).

117. Beckett, letter to Avigdor Arikha on Giacometti's theory of failure, quoted in Atik 2001: 83.

118. Beckett, letter to Thomas McGreevy, *c.*18 to 25 July 1930 (SBL1, 33). The Schopenhauer influence is well known; see Tonning 2011 for a survey.

119. James Knowlson mentions Pope's lines in discussing Beckett and theodicy (Knowlson 1997: 68).

120. See Schopenhauer 1969: 260; compare SBPD, 19, on the 'boredom of living'.

121. For crucifixion imagery in Beckett, see Ackerley and Gontarski 2004: 114–15.

122. Beckett, quoted in Juliet 2009: 16, 39.

123. Darwin, letter to Asa Gray, 22 May 1860, quoted in Cosslett 1984: 8.

124. Beckett, letter to Thomas MacGreevy, 8 September 1934 (SBL1, 222–3).

125. SBL1, 222–3. For a discussion of this letter, see Tonning 2007: 44–6.

126. I identified this source in Tonning 2009: 119.

127. Johnson, quoted in Tonning 2009: 119–20, my italics. Beckett recorded only the first paragraph in his notes, but the poison/antidote contrast clearly stayed with him.

128. For Beckett's notes, see Frost and Maxwell 2006: 39–49.

129. Beckett, 'Dante and the Lobster' (in Beckett 2010a: 16). See Ackerley and Gontarski 2004: 475, for a list of references, including in *Happy Days* and *The Lost Ones*. Beckett also used the phrase 'on the qui vive' in a draft towards *Play*.

130. The lines are *Inferno* III 34–6, 40–2, 46–51, 64–9. See Caselli, 2005: 72; my discussion here draws on Caselli's, and all Dante references in my text have been identified in her book.

131. For a guide, see Ackerley and Gontarski 2004: 46–8.

132. Beckett, German Diary entry, 18 January 1937, quoted in Knowlson 1997: 247.

133. Garin Dowd (1998) first connected Leibniz and *How It Is*. For an overview of 'Beckett's Leibniz', see Tonning 2007, ch. 6 (which grounds the concepts used in this discussion in Beckett's reading).

134. Eliot, 'Dante' (1929), quoted in Mangianello 1980: 70. Compare the ironic juxtaposition of 'Beatrice and the brothel' in SBDr, 42.

135. See Reynolds 1981, ch. 3 for a full discussion of the rose imagery.

136. Beckett, letter to Thomas McGreevy, 21 February 1938, quoted in Weller 2009a: 40.

137. See Lewis 2010, for a wider treatment of Jamesian religious experience in modernism.

138. For Beckett's 'dud mystics', see Zurbrugg 1988: 145–72, 190–216.

139. This translation of Beckett's German is given in Tonning 2007: 184–5.

140. This source is identified in Nixon 2011: 219, n. 20.

141. For a discussion of the mystical 'eye' in Beckett, see Tonning 2010.

142. See Griffin 2007, especially chs 3–4. For comments on Heidegger, see Griffin 2007: 321–4.

143. Heidegger, 'What Is Metaphysics', quoted in Wolfe 2013: 113–14.

144. However, see Weller 2009b for a discussion. My claim is that even if Beckett did read Heidegger, their work is still antithetical.

145. Beckett, German Diary entries 20 December 1936 and 15 January 1937, quoted in Knowlson 1997: 238, 245. See also Nixon 2011, ch. 5.

146. For a discussion of this theme in Heidegger, see Wolfe 2010, ch. 4; this interesting material is only available in her DPhil thesis.

147. Beckett, German Diary entry, 19 November 1936, quoted in Knowlson 1997: 235.

148. For a discussion of Heidegger and Rilke, see Wolfe 2013: 53–9. Another favourite of Heidegger's ably treated by Wolfe in this same section is Friedrich Hölderlin. Those insisting on a significant Heidegger influence upon Beckett should compare their readings of these two poets; and might continue with an exploration of their respective uses of the pre-Socratics.

149. See Feldman 2006: 32–8, for a discussion of Beckett's pre-Socratic sources.

150. Beckett, letter to Alan Schneider, 21 November 1957, in Harmon 1999: 23.

151. Beckett, letter to Mary Manning, 11 July 1937; quoted in Knowlson 1997: 270.

152. RUL MS 3461/2, 99, quoted in Tonning 2009: 117. These prayers are consecutive in Beckett's notes, but not in the George Birkbeck Hill edition of the *Prayers and Meditations* that Beckett read (cf. Hill 1897: 31, 34).

153. Of course, leafing through the indexed pages for 'Christianity' in the *Oxford Handbook* reveals other incidental references, chiefly to obvious figures like Eliot, but no *systematic* discussion of 'Modernism and Christianity'. Naturally, this does not reflect on the many strong surveys of individual areas presented there, but the volume as a whole does indicate a certain trend within the field of Modernism studies.

BIBLIOGRAPHY

Archives

David Jones collection, National Library of Wales, Aberystwyth.
J. H. Oldham collection (Moot Papers), New College Library, University of Edinburgh.
Ezra Pound collection, Beinecke Library, Yale University.

Works Cited

Bibles

The Holy Bible. 1611. King James Authorized Version.
The Holy Bible; Translated from the Latin Vulgate; Diligently Compared with the Hebrew, Greek, and Other Editions, in Divers Languages: The Whole Revised and Diligently Compared with the Latin Vulgate. 1857. Dublin: James Duffy. [Quoted in Chapter 2 only.]

General Works

Ackerley, C. J. 2005. *Obscure Locks, Simple Keys: The Annotated Watt.* Tallahassee: Journal of Beckett Studies Books.

Ackerley, C. J., and S. E. Gontarski. 2004. *The Grove Companion to Samuel Beckett.* New York: Grove Press.

Aldritt, Keith. 2003. *David Jones: Writer and Artist.* London: Constable.

Allitt, Patrick. 1997. *Catholic Converts: British and American Intellectuals Turn to Rome.* Ithaca and London: Cornell University Press.

Aquinas, Thomas. 2008. *Summa Theologica.* Trans. Fathers of the English Dominican Province, 1920. Online edition http://www.newadvent.org/summa/3078.htm.

Armstrong, Charles. 2013. *Reframing Yeats: Genre, Allusion, and History.* London: Bloomsbury Academic.

Asher, Kenneth. 1995. *T. S. Eliot and Ideology.* Cambridge: Cambridge University Press.

Atik, Anne. 2001. *How It Was: A Memoir of Samuel Beckett.* London: Faber and Faber.

Auden, W. H. 1994. *Collected Poems.* Reprint: 2nd edn 1991. Ed. Edward Mendelson. London: Faber and Faber.

——2002. *Prose: Volume II: 1939–1948.* Ed. Edward Mendelson. Princeton, NJ: Princeton, University Press.

——2008. *Prose: Volume III: 1949–1955.* Ed. Edward Mendelson. Princeton, NJ: Princeton University Press.

———2010. *Prose: Volume IV: 1956–1962*. Ed. Edward Mendelson. Princeton, NJ: Princeton University Press.

Bacigalupo, Massimo. 2001. 'Ezra Pound's "European Paideuma"'. *Paideuma* 30.1–2 (Spring and Fall): 225–45.

Bailey, Iain. forthcoming. *Samuel Beckett and the Bible*. London: Bloomsbury Academic.

Bauman, Zygmunt. 1991. *Modernity and Ambivalence*. Cambridge: Polity.

Beckett, Samuel. 1957. *Murphy*. New York: Grove Press.

———1990. *The Complete Dramatic Works*. London: Faber and Faber.

———1992. *Dream of Fair to Middling Women*. Dublin: Black Cat Press.

———1995. *The Complete Short Prose, 1929–1989*. Ed. S. E. Gontarski. New York: Grove Press.

———1996. *How It Is*. London: Calder.

———1997. *Molloy. Malone Dies. The Unnamable*. London: Calder.

———1999. *Beckett's 'Dream' Notebook*. Ed. John Pilling. Reading: BIF.

———1999. *Proust and Three Dialogues with Georges Duthuit*. London: Calder.

———2001. *Disjecta: Miscellaneous Writings and a Dramatic Fragment*. Ed. Ruby Cohn London: Calder.

———2009a. *Company, Ill Seen Ill Said, Worstward Ho*. Ed. Dirk Van Hulle. London: Faber and Faber.

———2009b. *Watt*. Ed. Chris Ackerley. London: Faber and Faber.

———2010a. *More Pricks Than Kicks*. Ed. Cassandra Nelson. London: Faber and Faber.

———2010b. *The Letters of Samuel Beckett*, Vol. 1: 1929–1940. Ed. Martha Dow Fehsenfeld and Lois More Overbeck. Cambridge: Cambridge University Press.

———2011. *The Letters of Samuel Beckett*, Vol. 2: 1941–1956. Ed. Martha Dow Fehsenfeld and Lois More Overbeck. Cambridge: Cambridge University Press.

———2012. *The Collected Poems of Samuel Beckett: A Critical Edition*. Ed. Seán Lawlor and John Pilling. London: Faber and Faber.

Berger, Peter. 1967. *The Sacred Canopy: Elements of a Sociological Theory of Religion*. London: Doubleday.

Berman, Marshall. 1982. *All That Is Solid Melts into Air. The Experience of Modernity*. London: Verso.

Bowler, Peter J. 1988. *The Non-Darwinian Revolution: Reinterpreting a Historical Myth*. Baltimore and London: Johns Hopkins University Press.

———2001. *Reconciling Science and Religion: The Debate in Early Twentieth-Century Britain*. Chicago and London: University of Chicago Press.

Brooke-Rose, Christine. 1971. *A ZBC of Ezra Pound*. Berkeley and Los Angeles: University of California Press.

Brooker, Peter, Andrzej Gasiorek, Deborah Longworth and Andrew Thacker, eds. 2010. *The Oxford Handbook of Modernisms*. Oxford: Oxford University Press.

Brown, Keith. 2008. *Sightings: Selected Literary Essays*. Ed. Erik Tonning. Bern: Peter Lang.

Bryden, Mary. 1998. *Samuel Beckett and the Idea of God*. London: Macmillan.

Bühler, Pierre. 2008. 'Tertullian: The Teacher of the *credo quia absurdum*'. In *Kierkegaard and the Patristic and Medieval Traditions*. Ed. Jon Stewart. Aldershot: Ashgate: 131–42.

Bush, Ronald. 1976. *The Genesis of Ezra Pound's Cantos*. Princeton, NJ: Princeton University Press.

———2010. '"An Easy Commerce of the Old and New?": Recent Eliot Scholarship'. *Modernism/modernity* 17.3 (September): 677–81.

Campbell, Joseph, and Henry M. Robinson. 1944. *A Skeleton Key to Finnegans Wake: Unlocking James Joyce's Masterwork*. New York: Harcourt, Brace.

Caselli, Daniela. 2005. *Beckett's Dantes: Intertextuality in the Fiction and Criticism*. Manchester: Manchester University Press.

Clements, Keith. 2010. *The Moot Papers: Faith, Freedom and Society 1938–1944*. London and New York: T&T Clark.

Cheng, Vincent J. 1995. *Joyce, Race, and Empire*. Cambridge: Cambridge University Press.

Cosslett, Tess, ed. 1984. *Science and Religion in the Nineteenth Century*. Cambridge: Cambridge University Press.

Cunningham, Conor. 2002. *Genealogy of Nihilism*. London and New York: Routledge.

Dante Aligheri. 1982. *The Divine Comedy of Dante Aligheri*. Trans. Allen Mandelbaum (dual text edition). New York: Bantam Books.

de la Taille, Maurice. 1934. *The Mystery of Faith*. Trans. John O'Connor. London: Sheed and Ward.

Dilworth, Thomas. 1979. *The Liturgical Parenthesis of David Jones*. Ipswich: Golgonooza Press.

———1986. 'David Jones and Fascism'. *Journal of Modern Literature* 13.1 (March): 149–62.

———1988. *The Shape of Meaning in the Poetry of David Jones*. Toronto: University of Toronto Press.

———2012. *David Jones in the Great War*. London: Enitharmon Press.

Dowd, Garin. 1998. 'Nomadology: Reading the Beckettian Baroque'. *Journal of Beckett Studies* 8.1: 15–49.

Eliot, T. S. 1928. 'The Literature of Fascism'. *Criterion* 8 (December): 280–90.

———1930. 'Poetry and Propaganda'. *The Bookman* 70 (February 1930): 595–602.

———1933. *After Strange Gods: A Primer of Modern Heresy*. London: Faber and Faber.

———1973. *The Complete Poems and Plays of T. S. Eliot*. Reprint: 1st edn 1969. London: Faber and Faber.

———1975. *Selected Prose*. Ed. Frank Kermode. London: Faber and Faber.

———1976. *Christianity and Culture: The Idea of a Christian Society and Notes towards the Definition of Culture*. San Diego, New York and London: Harcourt.

———1999. *Selected Essays*. London: Faber and Faber.

———2009. *The Letters of T. S. Eliot. Volume 2: 1923–1925*. Ed. Valerie Eliot and John Haffenden. London: Faber and Faber.

———2012. *The Letters of T. S. Eliot. Volume 3: 1926–1927*. Ed. Valerie Eliot and John Haffenden. London: Faber and Faber.

———2013. *The Letters of T. S. Eliot. Volume 4: 1928–1929*. Ed. Valerie Eliot and John Haffenden. London: Faber and Faber.

Emery, Clark. 1969. *Ideas into Action: A Study of Pound's Cantos*. Reprint: 1st edn 1958. Coral Gables, FL: University of Miami Press.

Feldman, Matthew. 2006. *Beckett's Books: A Cultural History of Samuel Beckett's 'Interwar Notes'*. London and New York: Continuum.

———2012. 'The "Pound Case" in Historical Perspective: An Archival Overview'. *Journal of Modern Literature* 35.2 (Winter): 83–97.

———2013. *Ezra Pound's Fascist Propaganda 1935–1945*. Basingstoke: Palgrave.

Fordham, Finn. forthcoming. 'How "modernism" changed on or around the Vatican's *Oath against Modernism*, September 1910'. *Literature & History*, third series, 22.1.

Frazer, James. 1976. *The Golden Bough: A Study in Magic and Religion*. London: Macmillan.

Frost, Everett, and Jane Maxwell. 2006. 'Catalogue of "Notes Diverse Holo[graph]"'. *Samuel Beckett Today/Aujourd'hui* 16: 15–173.

Gentile, Emilio. 2000. 'The Sacralisation of Politics: Definitions, Interpretations and Reflections on the Question of Secular Religion and Totalitarianism'. Trans. Robert Mallett. *Totalitarian Movements and Political Religions* 1.1 (Summer):18–55.

Gillespie, Michael Allen. 2009. *The Theological Origins of Modernity*. Reprint: 1st edn 2008. Chicago and London: University of Chicago Press.

Griffin, Roger. 2007. *Modernism and Fascism. The Sense of a Beginning under Mussolini and Hitler*. London: Palgrave.

Hanson, Ellis. 1997. *Decadence and Catholicism*. Cambridge, MA and London: Harvard University Press.

Harmon, Maurice, ed. 1999. *No Author Better Served: The Correspondence of Samuel Beckett and Alan Schneider*. Cambridge, MA and London: Harvard University Press.

Hart, David Bentley. 2004. *The Beauty of the Infinite: The Aesthetics of Christian Truth*. Reprint: 1st edn 2003. Grand Rapids, Michigan: Eerdmans.

Hill, George Birkbeck, ed. 1897. *Johnsonian Miscellanies*, Vol. 1. Oxford: Clarendon Press.

Inge, William. 1919. 'Catholicism and the Future' (Review of Maude Petre, *Modernism*), *Times Literary Supplement* (2 January).

Jain, Manju. 2004. *T. S. Eliot and American Philosophy*. Reprint: 1st edn 1992. Cambridge: Cambridge University Press.

James, William. 1982. *The Varieties of Religious Experience*. New York: Penguin.

Johnson, Philip. 2013. 'Is God Constitutional?' www.essentialism.net/is_god_unconstitutional.htm.

Johnson, Samuel. 2009. *The History of Rasselas, Prince of Abisinnia*. Oxford: Oxford University Press.

Jones, David. 1953. *The Anathemata*. London: Faber and Faber.

——1959. *Epoch and Artist: Selected Writings*. London: Faber and Faber.

——1978a. *In Parenthesis*. Reprint: 1st edn 1937. London: Faber and Faber.

——1978b. *The Dying Gaul and Other Writings*. London: Faber and Faber.

——1995. *The Sleeping Lord: And Other Fragments*. London: Faber and Faber.

Joyce, James. 1963. *Stephen Hero*. Ed. Herbert Cahoon, John J. Slocum and Theodore Spencer. New York: New Directions.

——1966. *Letters of James Joyce*, Vol. III. Ed. Richard Ellmann. New York: Viking.

——1993. *Ulysses. The 1922 Text*. Reprint: 1st edn 1922. Ed. Jeri Johnson. Oxford: Oxford University Press.

——2000. *Dubliners*. Reprint: 1st edn 1992. Ed. Terence Brown. London: Penguin Books.

——2008a. *A Portrait of the Artist as a Young Man*. Reprint: 1st edn 2000. Ed. Jeri Johnson. Oxford: Oxford University Press.

——2008b. *Occasional, Critical, and Political Writing*. Reprint: 1st edn 2000. Ed. Kevin Barry. Oxford: Oxford University Press.

Joyce, Stanislaus. 1962. *The Dublin Diary of Stanislaus Joyce*. Ed. George Harris Healey. London: Faber and Faber.

Juliet, Charles. 2009. *Conversations with Samuel Beckett and Bram Van Velde*. Trans. Tracy Cooke et al. Champaign and London: Dalkey Archive Press.

Julius, Anthony. 1995. *T.S. Eliot, Anti-Semitism and Literary Form*. Cambridge: Cambridge University Press.

Kermode, Frank. 2000. *The Sense of an Ending: Studies in the Theory of Fiction*. Reprint: 1st edn 1967. Oxford: Oxford University Press.

Kerr, Fergus. 1992. 'Simplicity Itself: Milbank's Thesis'. *New Blackfriars* 73.861 (June): 305–10.

Kirsch, Arthur. 2005. *Auden and Christianity*. New Haven and London: Yale University Press.

Knowlson, James. 1997. *Damned to Fame: The Life of Samuel Beckett*. Reprint: 1st edn 1996. London: Bloomsbury.

Koselleck, Reinhardt. 1988. *Critique and Crisis. Enlightenment and the Pathogenesis of Modern Society*. Oxford: Berg.

Kurlberg, Jonas. forthcoming. 'The Moot, the End of Civilisation, and the Re-birth of Christendom'. In *Modernism, Christianity, and Apocalypse*. Ed. Erik Tonning, Matthew Feldman and David Addyman. Leiden: Brill.

Lang, Frederick K. 1993. *Ulysses and the Irish God*. London and Toronto: Associated University Presses.

Larsen, Timothy. 2008. *Crisis of Doubt: Honest Faith in Nineteenth-Century England*. Oxford: Oxford University Press.

Lawrence, D. H. 1977. *Apocalypse*. Reprint: 1st Penguin edn 1974. London: Penguin.

Lernout, Geert. 2010. *Help My Unbelief: James Joyce and Religion*. London: Continuum.

Lewis, Pericles. 2010. *Religious Experience and the Modernist Novel*. Cambridge: Cambridge University Press.

Liebregts, Peter Th. M. G. 2004. *Ezra Pound and Neoplatonism*. Cranbury, NJ: Associated University Presses.

Livingston, James C. 2007. *Religious Thought in the Victorian Age: Challenges and Reconceptions*. New York and London: Continuum.

Mangianello, Dominic. 1980. *Joyce's Politics*. London, Boston and Henley: Routledge & Kegan Paul.

——1989. *T. S. Eliot and Dante*. New York: St Martin's Press.

Maritain, Jacques. 1923. *The Philosophy of Art [Art et scholastique]*. Trans. John O'Connor. Ditchling: S. Dominic's Press.

McAlonan, Pauline. 2006. 'Wrestling with Angels: T. S. Eliot, W. H. Auden, and the Idea of a Christian Poetics'. PhD thesis, McGill University.

McDiarmid, Lucy. 1990. *Auden's Apologies for Poetry*. Princeton, NJ: Princeton University Press.

Mendelson, Edward. 1981. *Early Auden*. New York: Farrar, Straus and Giroux.

——1999. *Later Auden*. New York: Farrar, Straus and Giroux.

Milbank, John. 2006. *Theology and Social Theory: Beyond Secular Reason*. 2nd edn. 1st edn 1990. Oxford: Blackwell Publishing.

Milbank, John, and Simon Oliver, eds. 2009. *The Radical Orthodoxy Reader*. London and New York: Routledge.

Miles, Jonathan and Derek Shiel. 2003. Reprint: 1st edn 1995. *David Jones: The Maker Unmade*. Bridgend: Seren.

Moi, Toril. 2006. *Henrik Ibsen and the Birth of Modernism: Art, Theater, Philosophy*. Oxford: Oxford University Press.

Niebuhr, Reinhold. 1964. *The Nature and Destiny of Man. A Christian Interpretation. Volume I. Human Nature*. Reprint: 1st edn 1941. New York: Charles Scribner's Sons.

Nietzsche, Friedrich. 2008. *On the Genealogy of Morals*. Trans. Douglas Smith. Reprint: 1st edn 1996. Oxford: Oxford University Press.

Nixon, Mark. 2011. *Samuel Beckett's German Diaries 1936–1937*. London: Continuum.

Noon, William T. 1957. *Joyce and Aquinas*. New Haven: Yale University Press.

North, Michael. 1991. *The Political Aesthetic of Yeats, Eliot, and Pound.* Cambridge: Cambridge University Press.

Oldham, J. H. 1940. *The Resurrection of Christendom.* London: Sheldon Press.

Oliver, Simon. 2009. 'Introducing Radical Orthodoxy: From Participation to Late Modernity'. In *The Radical Orthodoxy Reader.* Ed. John Milbank and Simon Oliver. London: Routledge: 3–27.

Ottomeyer, Hans. forthcoming. 'The Reason of Nature. Revolution of Principles around 1900'. In *Modernism, Christianity, and Apocalypse.* Ed. Erik Tonning, Matthew Feldman and David Addyman. Leiden: Brill.

Owen, Alex. 2004. *The Place of Enchantment: British Occultism and the Culture of the Modern.* Chicago and London: University of Chicago Press.

Paley, William. 2008. *Natural Theology.* Oxford: OUP World Classics.

Perl, Jeffrey. 1984. *The Tradition of Return. The Implicit History of Modern Literature.* Princeton, NJ: Princeton University Press.

Pickstock, Catherine. 1998. *After Writing: On the Liturgical Consummation of Philosophy.* Oxford: Blackwell.

Pitcher, George. 1907. 'The September Encyclical of Pius X'. *The New Age,* new series, 1.24 (10 October).

Pound, Ezra. 1950. *The Letters of Ezra Pound 1907–1941.* Ed. D. D. Paige. New York: Harcourt, Brace & World.

——1953. *The Spirit of Romance.* Reprint: 1st edn 1929. New York: New Directions.

——1968. *Literary Essays of Ezra Pound.* Reprint: 2nd edn 1960. London: Faber and Faber.

——1970a. *Guide to Kulchur.* New York: New Directions.

——1970b. *Jefferson and/or Mussolini.* New York: Liveright.

——1973. *Ezra Pound: Selected Prose 1909–1965.* Ed. William Cookson. London: Faber and Faber.

——1991. *Ezra Pound's Poetry and Prose: Contributions to Periodicals,* prefaced and arranged by Lea Baechler, A. Walton Litz and James Longenbach, 10 vols. [Addenda and Index in vol. XI]. New York and London: Garland.

——1996a. *The Cantos of Ezra Pound.* Reprint: 1st pbk edn 1996. New York: New Directions.

——1996b. *Machine Art & Other Writings: The Lost Thought of the Italian Years.* Ed. Maria Luisa Ardizzone. Durham and London: Duke University Press.

——1998. *'I Cease Not to Yowl': Ezra Pound's Letters to Olivia Rossetti Agresti.* Ed. Demetres P. Tryphonopoulos and Leon Surette. Urbana and Chicago: University of Illinois Press.

Purdy, Dwight H. 1994. *Biblical Echo and Allusion in the Poetry of W. B. Yeats: Poetics and the Art of God.* London: Associated University Presses.

Redman, Tim. 1991. *Ezra Pound and Italian Fascism.* Cambridge: Cambridge University Press.

Reynolds, Mary T. 1981. *Joyce and Dante: The Shaping Imagination.* Princeton, NJ: Princeton University Press.

Richards, Robert J. 2008. *Tragic Sense of Life: Ernst Haeckel and the Struggle Over Evolutionary Thought.* Chicago: University of Chicago Press.

Rinaldi, Andrea. forthcoming. '"Till Armageddon, No Shalam, No Shalom." Ezra Pound and the Consecration of Politics in the Italian Press During WWII'. In *Modernism, Christianity, and Apocalypse.* Ed. Erik Tonning, Matthew Feldman and David Addyman. Leiden: Brill.

Robichaud, Paul. 2007. *Making the Past Present: David Jones, the Middle Ages, & Modernism*. Washington, DC: Catholic University of America Press.

Sass, Louis A. 1992. *Madness and Modernism: Insanity in the Light of Modern Art, Literature, and Thought*. New York: Basic Books.

Schuchard, Ronald. 1999. *Eliot's Dark Angel: Intersections of Life and Art*. Oxford: Oxford University Press.

Schloesser, Stephen. 2005. *Jazz Age Catholicism: Mystic Modernism in Postwar Paris 1919–1933*. Toronto: University of Toronto Press.

Schmidt, Leigh Eric. 2003. 'The Making of Modern "Mysticism"'. *Journal of the American Academy of Religion* 71.2: 273–302.

Schopenhauer, Arthur. 1969. *The World as Will and Representation*, Vol. 1. Trans. E. F. J. Payne. New York: Dover.

Shaw, Bernard. 1907. 'The New Theology', *Christian Commonwealth* (23 and 27 May).

Sider, Robert D. 1980. 'Credo Quia Absurdum?' *Classical World* 73 (April–May): 417–19.

Spalding, Francis. 1980. *Roger Fry: Art and Life*. Berkeley and Los Angeles: University of California Press.

Spurr, Barry. 2010. *'Anglo-Catholic in Religion': T. S. Eliot and Christianity*. Cambridge: Lutterworth Press.

Staudt, Kathleen Henderson. 1994. *At the Turn of a Civilization: David Jones and Modern Poetics*. Ann Arbor: University of Michigan Press.

Sudlow, Brian. 2011. *Catholic Literature and Secularisation in France and England, 1880–1914*. Manchester: Manchester University Press.

Surette, Leon. 1979. *A Light from Eleusis: A Study of Ezra Pound's Cantos*. Oxford: Clarendon Press.

——1993. *The Birth of Modernism. Ezra Pound, T. S. Eliot, W. B. Yeats and the Occult*. Montreal and Kingston: McGill-Queen's University Press.

——1999. *Pound in Purgatory: From Economic Radicalism to Anti-Semitism*. Urbana and Chicago: University of Illinois Press.

Taylor, Charles. 2007. *A Secular Age*. Cambridge, MA and London: Belknap Press of Harvard University Press.

Terrell, Carroll F. 1993. *A Companion to the Cantos of Ezra Pound*. Berkeley, Los Angeles and London: University of California Press.

Tonning, Erik. 2007. *Samuel Beckett's Abstract Drama: Works for Stage and Screen, 1962–1985*. Bern: Peter Lang.

——2009. 'Beckett's Unholy Dying: From *Malone Dies* to *The Unnamable*'. In *Beckett and Death*. Ed. Steven Barfield, Matthew Feldman and Philip Tew. London and New York: Continuum: 106–27.

——2010. '"Nor by the eye of flesh nor by the other": Fleshly, Creative and Mystical Vision in Late Beckett'. *Samuel Beckett Today/Aujourd'hui* 22: 223–39.

——2011. '"I am not reading philosophy": Beckett and Schopenhauer'. *Sofia Philosophical Review* 5.1: 19–44.

Tryphonopolous, Demetres P., and Stephen J. Adams, eds. 2005. *The Ezra Pound Encyclopedia*. Westport, CT and London: Greenwood Press.

Van Gogh, Vincent. 2003. *The Letters of Vincent Van Gogh*. London: Penguin.

Vassenden, Eirik. 2012. *Norsk Vitalisme: Litteratur, ideologi og livsdyrking 1890–1940*. Oslo: Scandinavian University Press.

Villis, Tom. 2013. *British Catholics and Fascism: Religious Identity and Political Extremism between the Wars*. London: Palgrave.

Walzl, Florence L. 1961. 'Patterns of Paralysis in Joyce's *Dubliners*: A Study of the Original Framework'. *College English* 22.4: 221–8.

Ward, Elizabeth. 1983. *David Jones: Myth-maker*. Manchester: Manchester University Press.

Weller, Shane. 2009a. '"Orgy of false being life in common": Beckett and the Politics of Death'. In *Beckett and Death*. Ed. Steven Barfield, Matthew Feldman and Philip Tew. London and New York: Continuum: 31–49.

——2009b. 'Phenomenologies of the Nothing: Democritus, Heidegger, Beckett'. In *Beckett and Phenomenology*. Ed. Matthew Feldman and Ulrika Maude. London and New York: Continuum: 39–55.

——2011. *Modernism and Nihilism*. London: Palgrave.

Williams, Charles. 1939. *The Descent of the Dove: A Short History of the Holy Spirit in the Church*. London: Religious Book Club.

Wolfe, Judith. 2010. 'Heidegger's Secular Eschatology: Eschatological Thought in Martin Heidegger's Early Work, 1909–29 and beyond'. DPhil thesis, Oxford University.

——2013. *Heidegger's Secular Eschatology*. Oxford: Oxford University Press.

Wood, Diana. 2004. *Medieval Economic Thought*. Cambridge: Cambridge University Press.

Woolf, Virginia. 1975–80. *The Letters of Virginia Woolf*. Ed. Nigel Nicolson and Joanne Trautmann. San Diego: Harcourt Brace Jovanovich.

——2002. *Moments of Being: Autobiographical Writings*. Ed. Jeanne Schulkind. London: Pimlico.

Wright, T. R. 2000. *D. H. Lawrence and the Bible*. Cambridge: Cambridge University Press.

Zurbrugg, Nicholas. 1988. *Beckett and Proust*. Gerrards Cross: Colin Smythe.

INDEX

Printed and bound by CPI Group (UK) Ltd, Croydon, CR0 4YY